AF539192

PERSPECTIVES OF TRIBAL EDUCATION

PERSPECTIVES OF TRIBAL EDUCATION

Editors

Prof. Dhananjay Lokhande

Professor

Director and Head

Pune University Bulletin

&

Dr. P. Viswanadha Gupta

Assistant Professor

Dept. of Adult, Continuing Education & Extension

University of Pune

Pune (India)

DPH

DISCOVERY PUBLISHING HOUSE PVT. LTD.

NEW DELHI-110 002

Published by:
Tilak Wasan
DISCOVERY PUBLISHING HOUSE PVT. LTD.
4383/4B, Ansari Road, Darya Ganj
New Delhi-110 002 (India)
Phone : +91-11-23279245, 43596064-65
Fax : +91-11-23253475
E-mail : discoverypublishinghouse@gmail.com
sales@discoverypublishinggroup.com
parul.wasan@gmail.com
web : www.discoverypublishinggroup.com

***First Edition:* 2014**

ISBN: 978-93-5056-482-0

Perspectives of Tribal Education

Printed at:
Dynamic Printers
Delhi

Preface

Adivasis are the original inhabitants, who still love relatively in isolation of hills and forests. They are excluded from the mainstream population. Gandhiji said that, "Adivasis economic conditions are worse than that of Harijans who have long been victims of neglect on the part of the so called high classes". Even after India's independence, the tribals are still struggling hard to eke out their livelihood and live in extreme poverty condition. Majority of tribal population stand below poverty line and unable to meet their basic prime need of food and encountered with malnutrition, morbidity and mortality. The other area of their alienation is their culture. Most people seem to think of as the externals of dance and song. This gives the 'mainstream' the justification it needs to view them as communities of happy go lucky persons, who are not capable of developing themselves. To them their culture is a value system, whose externals may change but the core remains sacred. It is essentially a system based on the values of equity, renewability of the natural resources and respect for the whole community, past, present and future. The value system is the core of their identity. Many of them have been using it as a rally rallying point in mobilization against their exploitation.

Tribes in India still live in isolation and extreme poverty condition. Gandhiji's thought of upliftment of Adivasis is more appropriate strategy for Tribal Development. The ideology also incorporated in the Indian Constitution in providing certain safeguards and provisions for the upliftment and development of tribal communities. However, still the tribals are encountered with the problems like poverty, illiteracy, food insecurity, indebtedness, land alienation, malnutrition, morbidity and early deaths, due to scanty of resources in their habitats.

The development among the tribal communities taking place in a slow pace manner due to lack of commitment on the part of development agencies and non-participation of the aboriginals in the on-going development process. So far large majority of tribals are not fulfilled with the basic needs through the government initiated development programmes, moreover, they are denied to enjoy the rights over the land and forest resources of natural environment in which they inhabits. These are also considered to be root causes for the unrest among the tribals and a number of land and forest disputes arises in recent time. In this context the editors bringing out this edited volume on Perspectives of Tribal Education.

We express our sincere thanks to all faculty members of the department and out regards to the authors who have been accepted the invitation and contributed papers.

P. Viswanadha Gupta
Dhananjay Lokhande

Contents

1

Need of Peoples' Participation in Primary Education
Blockage and Strategies

1. Prof. B. S. Vasudeva Rao
2. Dr. P. Viswanadha Gupta

Free and compulsory education to all children up to the age of fourteen years is the Constitutional commitment in India. At the time of adoption of the Constitution in 1950, the aim was to achieve the goal of *Universalisation of Elementary Education* (UEE) within the next ten years *i.e.* by 1960. Keeping in view the educational facilities available in the country at that time, the goal was far too ambitious to achieve within a short span of ten years. Hence, the target date was shifted a number of times. Till 1960, all efforts were focused on provision of schooling facilities. It was only after the near realisation of the goal of access that other components of UEE, such as universal enrolment and retention, started receiving attention of planners and policy-makers. But, in spite of the Herculean

1. Principal Investigator, UGC Major Research Project, Department of Education, Andhra University, Visakhapatnam. E-mail: bandaru.vasu @gmail.com
2. Assistant Professor, Department of Adult, Continuing Education and Extension, University of Pune, Pune - 411 007. Email: pvgupta@ unipune.ac.in

efforts these results are not fruitful because of non-participation of stakeholders and related groups. Hence, the study was taken up in east Godawari district to identify the causes for non-participation of community and stakeholders. Strategies to strengthen the primary education were developed with the responses from the primary teachers for effective people's participation.

The better functioning of the primary schools only possible not only with the school staff but also involvement and co-operation of school education committee, community, mid-day meal agency, students, parents, higher officials of the school administration, political leaders and social activists. The positive attitudes and participation of these people have an impact on functioning of the school. Hence, opinion was gathered from respondents' (primary teachers) about pupils co-operation constrains they are facing from the people and practiced suggestions to over come these problems in a open ended question form.

School Education Committee

The School Education Committee was established by the government with a view to strength functioning of the school. The School Education Committee is consists five members from parents by following reservation system and village Sarpanch as Chairmen and Head Master acts as convenor. All the financial operation including mid-day meal programme will be operated by chairmen and Head Master. The mid-day meal agency operates as per the instructions of the School Education Committee. The implementation of mid-day meal scheme was entrusted to the selected local Indira Kranthi Group (DWACRA).

Problems faced from School Education Committees

1. The involvement of School Education Committee members is not as per the expectation. They will not feel responsibility about functioning and improvement of school development and functioning.
2. Their co-operation is meagre in school development but act as authoritative in all matters.

3. The School Education Committee meetings are not regularly conducted because of the absence of the members.
4. Apathy, ignorance and illiteracy of the members are also the factors for their less involvement in the school functioning.
5. The guidance of the government is that School Education Committee members are to be elected by the parents but the interference of political party members SEC will be appointed on nomination.
6. The committee members are not feeling responsible and behave as neutrals in critical issues.

Suggestions for Improvement

1. Minimum Educational Qualification has to fix to become a member of a School Education Committee.
2. Political interference is to be minimized.
3. Training programmes to be organized to members regarding their duties and functions in management and functioning of the school.

Community and Parents

In village setting any activity will be depending up on the attitude and co-operation of the people. The Rajiv Vidya Mission (SSA) included the concept of people's participation in the implementation and functioning of primary education at field situation. The rural people feel that they are powerless. They are also ignorant of law and welfare measures provided by the Government. Rural people do not have forum to assist them in securing redressal for their grievances. Illiteracy is also one of the major hindrances for participation (Vasudeva Rao, 2004). The causes for their low participation in school activity are listed as:

1. The local community has negative opinion about government schools in comparison with corporate schools.

2. Grama Sabha has no role in school activity because political dictatorship.
3. Illiteracy, poverty, traditional customs and beliefs influence the community for not enrolling their children, in schools particularly girl-child.
4. Community feels that by sending to school, they will loose one helping hand both in house hold activity and in their occupation.
5. Alcoholism, indifferent attitude, influence and fear from land lords are the main barriers for non-participation of community in school functioning.

Suggestions

1. Steps to be taken to create community awareness regarding importance of education and all are equal by birth.
2. Co-ordination and co-operation between teachers and community is to be facilitated.

Mid-day Meal Implementation Agency

The national programme for nutritional support to primary education (1995) provides food grains/cooked meals to children in primary classes along with schooling. The local community is also responsible in the implementation of the programme.

1. The agency is not providing balancing diet and providing cheap quality of food due to insufficient budget allotment and interference of vested control groups.
2. The quality and quantity supplied by the agency is not as per the guidelines of the government. The insufficient food made the children to depend on home food results discontinuation from schooling.
3. The influence, favouritism and control of local political leaders are more significant on the agency members.

Suggestions

1. Consolidated honorarium should be provided for the agency workers so that they will work with satisfaction.

2. The mid-day meal agency maximum term is to be fixed for two years. At present the agency which nominated once, continues due to patronage of leaders or School Education Committee.
3. At present, the agencies are nominated to provide mid-day meal to the students by local IKP group. Majority of the respondents feel it is giving scope for administrative influence on the agency, may be results decreasing quantity of food to be provided to the children. Hence, the system is not suggestive.
4. There is necessity to increase the rates (cost per student) fixed for mid-day meal, because of cost inflation.
5. Further, the workers of mid-day meal agency to be trained on health, hygiene, sanitation and also on preparation of balanced diet.

Students

The Sarva Siksha Abhiyan (Rajiv Vidya Mission in Andhra Pradesh) programme was implemented for effective functioning of primary schools. The main stakeholders of the programme are students. Their presence and regular attendance to the school only helps to sustain the programme. The success or failure of the programme depends upon enrollement and retention of the students. Only positive environment in schooling helps to retain them. Hence, actual field problems encounted by the teachers and the problems and suggestion are noted here:

1. Irregularity and absenteeism is more specially before and after vacation.
2. Influence of television is also one of the noted factor, for pupils absence to the school.
3. In agriculture seasons, pupils may stay at home or in the field to assist parents.
4. The parents disinterest on children education is also one of the influencing factor on students to dropout from schooling.

Suggestions

1. Financial assistance as scholarships to be provided to minority and poor students in primary level.
2. The old system of detention is to be introduced.
3. The school administration shall to organize the learning in a joyful way
4. The reading, writing and learning material may be supplied to the students on free of cost belongs to below the poverty line families.

Higher Officials

The effectiveness of teachers is depending upon the positive attitude of officials', effective monitoring and supervision, timely payment of salaries and providing other benefits/facilities.

1. Higher officials are facing pressure from political leaders and teacher unions in their daily administrative matters. Many times authorities decision changes depending upon the leader influence especially in teacher transfers and sanction of financial assistance.

Suggestions

1. For better functioning of school two Mandal Education Officers are to be appointed one for academic and second officer for supervision. Instead of existing practice of one MEO.
2. More efforts to be taken to support teachers in providing guidance in daily work. The training and guidance is necessary to the teachers in their job situation.
3. Supervision and monitoring system has insufficient at present. There is urgent need to strengthen supervision in primary education.

Teachers' Problems

Teachers are key functionary of the primary education programme. Teachers are overburden with official works like census, ration card verification, follow up of pulse polio programme, election duties, deputation of teachers to SSA work, visiting of MEO's office, preparing the salary bills, maintain service register and so on are main factors for ineffective functioning in their teaching work. These other activities are made them to restrict their activity in encourageing people's participation in school development. Hence, opinion was elicited primary school teachers are over burdened with official works than teaching by open ended question form:

1. Involvement in mid-day meal implementation.
2. Appointment of primary teachers as invigilators in higher examination during school time.
3. Lack of proper accommodation in work place.
4. Primary teachers some times deputed to secondary school to teach for higher classes due to lack of qualified teachers in secondary schools.
5. The teachers are frequently asked to attend the meetings arranged by higher authorities and many are unnecessary to prime level teachers.
6. The higher officials asking about information repeatedly hampering class work.

Suggestions

1. Office assistant post should be created in primary schools and MEO office. This will helps the teachers to concentrate on class work.
2. The stay of the teachers at workplace has to be made mandatory.
3. Incentives to be sanctioned to the teachers who contributed for enrolment and retention of students.

Suggestion for Strengthening the Programme

The primary school teachers were asked to provide their suggestions for better implementation of primary education by involving community. The question was asked to elicit their opinion by field experience.

1. Regular monitoring and supervision of schools activities are important.

2. Making girl education is as community agenda.
3. Empowering teachers academically and professionally through by organizing effective in service trainings and orientation programmes.
4. Incentives for teachers who acquired higher qualification during job period.
5. Training programmes for School Education Committee, elected leaders and Mahila Groups to be organized about need of education for future development.
6. Special retention drives particularly in low retention areas during seasonal migration.
7. Ensuring enrolment of all children into schools from Anganwadi centres.
8. Residential accommodation for school staff.
9. Teacher-Student ration as 1:20 to be followed.
10. Other than teaching it is better not entrust any governmental programmes to the teachers.
11. Minimum Educational Qualification to be fixed to constitute in School Education Committee.
12. Anganwadi centres to be attached to primary schools.
13. Reintroduce of detention system.
14. School environment should be attractive and villagers co-operation is necessary to keep the premises clean and green.
15. It is suggestive to increase the teaching learning material grant to Rs. 1000/- per annum instead of existing Rs. 500/ - PA.
16. Presence of women teachers is mandatory in every primary school like some of the other states.
17. Every school must have with minimum facilities like water, toilets, playground, games and sports materials and so on.
18. Present examination system to be modified.
19. Encourage computer learning from primary level like corporate schools.

20. Kinder gardens class should be arranged in every primary schools.
21. Every primary school must have three teachers one office assistant and Ayah.
22. The office work other than teaching should be done out of school time by paying adequate honorarium.

The school environment will be effective only with people's participation. As per the responses, there is no evidence of people's co-operation. The findings observed from the study that lack of participation of community results, causes the prevalence of 35 per cent of illiteracy even after 63 years of Independence Hence, there is an urgent need from administrators, academicians and planners to develop the mechanism to encourage people's participation and create healthy environment on teacher's working environment.

Your education, if it is a vital thing, must shed its fragrance in your surroundings. You must devote a certain portion of your time daily to serving the people around in a practical manner. You must, therefore, be prepared to take the spade, the broomstick and basket. You must become voluntary scavengers of this holy place. That would be the richest part of your education, not learning by heart literary thesis.

— Mahatma Gandhi, M. K.

REFERENCES

Abdul Kalam, A. P. J. 68th *Convocation Address at Andhra University*, Visakhapatnam, 2000.

Agarwal, J. C. *Basic Ideas in Education*, Shipra Publications, Delhi, 2001.

Buch, M. B. (Ed.), *Fourth Survey of Research in Education*, N. C. E. R. T., Vol. 2, New Delhi, 1988.

Damle, Y. B. *The Role of the Teacher in a Developing Society*, Ruhela, S. P. (ed.), Sociology of Teaching Profession, Delhi, 1970.

Fiffner and Sher Wood, *Administrative Organization*, Prentice Hall of India, New Delhi.

Raghunath Sajaya, *Current Problems in Indian Education*, Dhanpat Rai and Sons, Jalandhar.

Rao, V. K. Reddy, R. S. *Resource of Effective Teaching* (Editor Vol.), Commonwealth Publishers, New Delhi, 1992.

Sunderaj (2007), Peoples Centred Development: An Overview, Published in Rural Development Strategies and Role of Institutions (Ed. Volume) The Associate Publishers, Ambalakatta, New Delhi, 2004.

Vasudeva Rao, B. S. *Evaluation Studies*, (Edited Volume), The Associate Publishers, Ambalakatta, New Delhi, 2004.

2

Educating Tribal Children in Eklavya Model Residential Schools

A Strategy for Tribal Empowerment: The Way Towards Holistic Development

1. Yagyanand Garhewal
2. Dr. Sambit Kumar Padhi

The tribes of India are scattered all over the country differ from one another in racial traits, social organization and cultural pattern, etc. Most of the tribal communities have their own dialects, most of them without script. There are, however, enclaves and groups, which have not been influenced by other languages, who hardly can understand the language of non-tribal population. This is the reason they are the most disadvantaged group in terms of educational development. One of the distinguishing features of the tribals is that majority of them live in scattered habitations located in interior, remote and inaccessible, hilly and forest areas of the country. More than 90 per cent of scheduled tribe workers are engaged in the primary sector or sector of economy related to the exploitation of the natural resources. In view of their socio-

1. Research Scholar, Department of Education Guru Ghasidas Vishwavidyalaya, Bilaspur, Chhattisgarh. E-mail: garhewalprakhar @gmail.com
2. Assistant Professor, Department of Education, Guru Ghasidas Vishwavidyalaya, Bilaspur, Chhattisgarh. E-mail: padhiggv@gmail.com

economic backwardness, geographical isolation and marginalization, the Constitution of India has incorporated specific provisions for promoting and safeguarding the interests for the tribals. Specifically article 46 of the constitution envisages that: "The state shall promote with special care the educational and economic interests of the scheduled tribes and protect them from social injustice and all forms of exploitation". There are further provisions in articles 14 and 15 of the constitution for affirmative state actions in their favour.

It is universally accepted that education is the basic input for sustainable development of people and nation. It is also well understood that no state or nation can prosper without the sound system of education. Realising the importance of education for a large, democratic and welfare country like India, Indian constitution enshrines certain provisions promising equality of educational opportunities for all. In pursuance of these provisions, State and Central Government have given wide attention for promotion of education among all categories in general and socially and culturally disadvantaged groups in particular. Despite of incentives and special care for the development of education amongst the tribes, the process of educational development has far from satisfactory.

Tribal Education

Education in India has historically been the property of the few. Since educational development took place within the framework of stratified social system. It has always been focused on the needs of the privileged ones. The status of education for various clientele groups is dependent upon their socio-political profile in a given society. The Indian society has over a period of time undergone a process of continuous degeneration, namely, from Varna Vyavastha to the caste system. The present day Indian society which interact within their own formations with the result that those with a high educational profile continue to be in an advantageous position and those who were disadvantaged once continue to remain so. Of these the scheduled Castes and Scheduled Tribes form the largest part. Education of tribals is an important task before the Government of India. Unfortunately the literacy rate of the tribal population is very low. The national literacy rate, of scheduled tribes, according to 2001 census, is 47.10 per cent, which is much lower than the national literacy rate, *i.e.* 64.84 per cent. Therefore an educational planning for such a vast group of individuals should aim at educating all its members in the school going age group. Education is in fact, an input not only for economic development of tribes but also for inner strength of the tribal communities. It also helps them in meeting the new challenges of life. Education of ST children is considered important, not only because of the Constitutional obligation but also as a crucial input for total development of tribal communities.

The tribal education is lagging behind the general population. Not only this, the extent and pace of education has also remain slow among the tribals. The reasons for this can be categorised as external, internal and socio-economic and psychological. The external constraints are related to the problems and difficulties at the policy level, planning, implementation and at administration level. Internal constraints refer to problems related to the school system, content, curriculum, medium of instruction, pedagogy, teacher-related problems, academic supervision and monitoring. The third set of problems related to social, economic and cultural background of tribals and the psychological problems of first generation learners.

At present there are near about 645 tribal groups, which constitute 8.2 per cent of India's total population. Nearly three fourth of India's S.T. Population is concentrated in seven states in central India *i.e.* Madhya pradesh, Maharashtra Orissa, Bihar, Gujarat, Rajasthan and Andhra Pradesh. Odisha occupies a prominent space in the tribal map of India. Comparison to other states of India. According to 2001 census, the ST population of the state is 8145081, which constitutes 8.08 per cent of the total population of the country and 22.13

per cent of the total population of the state. There are as many sixty-two varieties of tribes in this state out of which fourteen major tribes may be shorted out who have distnict cultures of their own and belong to separate racial and linguistic groups.

Table 2.1: Literacy Rate of ST Population of Orissa and India (in %)

Census Year	Orissa			India		
	Person	Male	Female	Person	Male	Female
1961	7.4	13.0	1.8	7.99	13.04	2.89
1971	9.5	16.4	2.6	10.89	17.09	4.58
1981	14.0	23.3	4.8	16.35	24.52	8.04
1991	22.31	34.44	10.21	29.6	40.65	18.19
2001	37.4	51.5	23.4	47.1	59.2	34.8

*Census of India, 1961-2001.

The state has experienced a phenomenal expansion of its elementary education system. The literacy of state rate has improved from 7.4 per cent in 1961 to 37.4 per cent by 2001, while in case of India it has been increased from 7.99 per cent to 47.1 per cent. In spite of physical facilities the literacy rate of the tribal in Orissa in challenging. More over quality of education in schools is a major challenge. (Table 2.1)

Table 2.2: Literacy Rate among Total and ST Population of Orissa by Sex (in %)

Census Year	Total Population			ST Population		
	Male	Female	Total	Male	Female	Total
1961	34.70	8.65	21.66	13.04	1.77	7.36
1971	38.29	13.92	26.18	16.30	2.58	9.46
1981	47.10	21.10	34.20	23.27	4.76	13.96
1991	63.09	34.68	49.09	34.44	10.21	22.31
2001	75.35	50.51	63.08	51.48	23.37	37.37
2011	82.40	64.36	73.45	NA	NA	NA

* Census of India, 1961-2001.

The literacy rate of the Scheduled Tribes is lagging far behind that of the overall literacy rates of the country. Table 2.2 indicates there is a huge gap in the literacy rate between the tribal and all categories.

Table 2.3: Literacy of the Scheduled Tribes of Orissa

Sl. No.	Year	Percentage of Literacy		Tribal Disparity
		Total	S.Ts.	
1.	1961	21.66	07.36	14.30
2.	1971	26.18	09.46	16.72
3.	1981	34.23	13.96	20.27
4.	1991	49.09	22.31	26.78
5.	2001	63.08	37.37	25.71

The tribal disparity in literacy had steadily increased from 1961 to 1991; and registered a marginal decrease in 2001. The magnitude of tribal-disparity is more than 25 per cent; and more so when there has been a steady growth of population. This tribal-disparity in literacy has serious socio-economic repercussions and must be minimized through pro-active literacy activities. (Table 2.3)

Table 2.4: Gender Gap in Literacy Rate of ST Population of India and Orissa (in %)

Census Year	India			Orissa		
	Male	Female	Gender Gap	Male	Female	Gender Gap
1961	13.04	2.89	10.15	13.04	1.77	11.27
1971	17.09	4.58	12.51	16.30	2.58	13.72
1981	24.52	8.04	16.48	23.27	4.76	18.51
1991	40.65	18.19	22.46	34.44	10.21	24.23
2001	59.17	34.76	24.41	51.48	23.37	28.11

* Census of India, 1961-2001.

Eklavaya Model Residential Schools: An over View

In pursuance to the Article – 46 of the constitutional obligation, the Central as well as State Governments have therefore laid much emphasis on the spread of education in tribal areas. Many special schemes have been formulated in order to attract tribal children to school. Ministry of Tribal Affairs has been implementing various schemes for promotion of educational development schemes of the tribal communities and improving the quality of life of Tribals like Ashram School, Hostels for Tribal Boys and Girls, Educational Complexes, Post Matric Scholarship, Book Bank Scheme etc. A New concept for educational development "Establishment of Model Residential Schools was launched during 1997-98 to provide quality education to the tribal students. It was decided by the Ministry of Tribal affairs to utilise a part of the funds under Article 275 (1) of the Constitution, for setting up of 100 Model Residential Schools from Class VI to XII in different tribal concentrated states of the Country. These Schools are to be operated in each States through an autonomous society formed for this purpose. In order to provide a uniform pattern of education in those schools and enable their students to compete effectively for higher education programmes (medical, technical etc.) These schools are affiliated to State Boards. The Model Residential Schools have been named as Eklavaya Model Residential Schools (EMRS) and envisaged on the lines of Navodaya Vidyalayas but with State centered management. The establishment of Model Residential School is one of the novel experiments to help the meritorious tribal student for providing quality education in the remote Tribal Area of the Country.

Objectives of EMRS

The objectives of setting of EMRS is to provide quality education up to secondary and Higher Secondary stage to Scheduled Tribe (ST) students in remote areas. This will enable the students avail the facilities of reservation in higher and professional educational courses as well as in higher level of jobs in Government and public sector undertakings and in private sectors but also to have access to the best opportunities in education at per with the non-ST population.

This would be Achieved by:

- Comprehensive physical, mental and socially relevant development of all student enrolled in each and every

EMRS. Students will be empowered to be change agent, beginning in their school, in their homes, in their village and finally in a larger context.

- Focus differentially on the educational support to be made available to those in Standards XI and XII, and those in standards VI to X, so that their distinctive needs can be mat.
- Support the annual running expenses in a manner that offers reasonable remuneration to the staff and upkeep of the facilities.
- Support the construction of infrastructure that provides education, physical, environmental and cultural needs of student life.

EMRS in Odisha

In Orissa as per the guidelines of Ministry of Tribal Affairs, Government of India, Ekalavya Model Tribal Residential Schools were started functioning since 2000-01. In its 12 years of functioning 13 EMRS have been established across the State covering total of 11 districts. Among them three EMRSs are in Sundargarh Districts on each in Mayurbhanj, Keonjhar, Nabarangpur, Koraput, Rayagada, Gajapati, Nuapada, Malkanagiri, Kandhamal and Jajpur Districts.

Future Perspectives

Education of tribals cannot be left to short-term Plan strategies. It is important that planners take a long-term view which is embedded in a meaningful policy frame-work. Following are some important points emerging from the review here.

- Emphasis should be on quality and equity rather than quantity as has been the case in the past. The prime focus should be on provision of quality education that makes tribal communities economically effective and independent.
- In the tribal context, it is essential that the school schedule be prepared as per local requirement rather than following a directive from the state as it has been found that vacations and holidays are planned without taking into consideration local contexts.

- Though it has been highlighted time and again, no concrete step has been taken to provide locally relevant material to tribal students. Availability of locally relevant materials will not only facilitate faster learning but also help children develop a sense of affiliation to school.
- In order to make education effective and sustainable, building partnership between the community and the government is important. Results from pilot projects in various states show that community partnership not only augments state expenditure on education but also guarantees supervision and monitoring, thus addressing an intractable problem for the state.
- Environment building is of immense importance in the context of educational development among tribal communities. Community awareness and community mobilization, which are its core elements, should receive adequate importance and attention.
- Decentralization of education management is another aspect that needs special consideration in the context of tribal areas. In fact, considering the geographical terrain and communication problems in tribal areas, it is crucial to restructure the existing system of educational management. Adaptation of structures such as school complexes and VECs to tribal areas needs carefull consideration.
- Skill development, competency building, and teachers motivation also need to be strengthened for sustaining educational development. The teacher should be made the centre of educational transformation, and therefore, must remain the primary facilitator.

Truly speaking, despite all attempts in the direction of the national goal-equality of opportunity, the result is yet to become satisfactory. The progress seems slow and most particularly very slow and discouraging in case of handicapped children. Sorting out handicapped children of different categories liked dumb, orthopaedically handicapped, blind, deaf and subnormal is, no doubt, a stupendous task. Besides, making of educational provision for their socio-economic development through the process of education is also very difficult. To surmount the problem of providing equality of opportunity, incentive measures are to be provided as well to be properly implemented. Administrative structure has to be overhauled with a strong will and determination. Various media, methods and materials are to be utilised to fulfil the special needs of the deprived and the handicapped children.

REFERENCES

Fishman, J. A. (1999), Hand Book of Language and Ethnic Identity, New York: OUP.

Kangas, T. S. (1999), Education of Minorities, New York: OUP.

Majumdar, D. N. (1958), Races and Culture in India, Bombay: Asia Publishing House.

National Policy on Education (1986), MHRD ,GOI, New Delhi.

Nehru, Jawaharlal (1954), 'Forward' to Elwin, V., Philosophy for Tribal Development, New Delhi.

Patnaik, N. (1982), Tribal Life in Orissa, Souvenir Orissa Sahitya Academy, Bhubaneswar.

Ratnaih (1977), Structural Constraints of Tribal Education, New Delhi: Sterling Publication.

Rout, P. C. (1989), Tribal Education in Orissa, Bhubaneswar: Eastern Graphics.

Sujatha, K (1994), Educational Development Among Tribes: A Study of Sub-Plan Areas in Andhra Pradesh, New Delhi: South Asian Publishers.

3

Role of Education in Tribal Empowerment

1. Dr. John S. Gaikwad

ABSTRACT

Tribal are the weakest of the weaker sections. During British period most of the pre-literate communities were kept away from literacy as well as formal education. After independence, measures were taken to integrate and develop the tribal and bring them in the mainstream. The various programmes for Tribal Development include the component of education. Literacy and level of education are two basic indicators of development achieved by a society. The literacy rate among the tribal population in Maharashtra State is less than the overall literacy rate for the general population. Similar trend is observed for the literacy rates of male and female tribal population. The data related to educational level indicates that the drop out rate is conspicuous after the primary level and again after secondary levels among majority of the Scheduled Tribes. At present there are about 1100 Ashram Schools in Maharashtra State.

1. Associate Professor, Department of Anthropology, University of Pune, Pune - 411 007.

Enrolment in Government Ashram Schools is preferred mostly because the admission makes the student eligible for free food and clothing, apart from free education. The parents do not prefer to admit their children in the nearby primary schools (day schools). The total number of female students enrolled is much less for all the standards. It is observed that the enrolment decreases from standard I to standard X. The drop-outs at an early stage can be attributed to the feeling of 'alienation' imposed by 'marathi' as the medium of instruction. Responsibilities of contribution in the income generation activities or helping the family are major reasons for drop-out. Early marriages contribute to the drop-out of girls. Many of the first generation learners are not capable of adjusting themselves with the structured set up of formal education. Educated children are considered to be a loss to the family.

The network of ashram schools should became effective, efficient and yield optimum results in terms of academic excellence and quality.

Awareness among the tribal about the importance and relevance of education would replace the apathy with pro-active enthusiasm for education of the children.

Prologue and Introduction

Tribal communities are the weakest of the weaker sections. One of the most distinct features of the tribal communities is their 'habitat', which usually is in deep interior forest with difficult terrain, in hilly or non hilly region. Taking into consideration their distinct culture and habitation, the British preferred to conveniently keep the tribal communities in isolation, on the pretext of protection of the tribal communities and preserving their culture. Unfortunately these factors kept these pre-literate communities away from literacy as well as formal Education (However, there are very few exceptions to this). With this, the tribal communities were kept away from the main stream.

After independence, it was decided to bring the tribal communities in the main stream. For bringing the tribal communities in the main stream, two different approaches were advocated:

(i) Assimilation and Development of Tribal communities.

(ii) Integration and Development of Tribal communities.

Preference has been given to an integrated approach for Tribal development. Prior to 1950, the Government of India had no direct programme for the education of the tribal communities. With the adoption of the Constitution, the promotion of education of Scheduled tribes has become a special responsibility of the Central as well as of the State Governments. Like all other sectors of socio-economic life, educationally, the tribal communities are at different levels of development (Ratha S. M. 1986).

Attempts were made to give a desired shape to the objectives of the development of the 'Scheduled Areas' by various administrative measures ranging from Block Development Programmes, Multipurpose Community Development Blocks and Integrated Tribal Development Projects under Tribal Sub Plan. The various development programmes implemented for Tribal Development included the equally important component of Education.

Education has the Potential for:

- human resource development;
- improvement of quality of life; and
- contribution in the process of planned social change.

Pandit Jawaharlal Nehru has delineated the 'Pancha-sheel' – goals/five fundamental principles for tribal development, (which have been mentioned by Pandit Jawaharlal Nehru, in his 'Foreword' to the second edition (1959) of 'Philosophy for NEFA', by Verrier Elwin.

The 'Pancha-sheel' – Five Fundamental Principles of Tribal Development are:

1. People should develop along the lines of their own genius and we should avoid imposing anything on them. We should try to encourage in every way their own traditional arts and culture.

2. Tribal rights in land and forests should be respected.
3. We should try to train and build up a team of their own people to do the work of administration and development. Some technical personnel from outside will, no doubt, be needed, especially in the beginning. But we should avoid introducing too many outsiders into tribal territory.
4. We should not over-administer these areas or overwhelm them with a multiplicity of schemes. We should rather work through, and not in rivalry to, their own social and cultural institutions.
5. We should judge results, not by statistics or the amount of money spent, but by the quality of human character that is evolved.

Pandit Jawaharlal Nehru advocated the need for 'psychological approach' for achieving 'psychological integration' (A New Deal for Tribal India – Report of the Scheduled Areas and Scheduled Tribes Commissions 1963). – (Quoted in Mathur H. M. 1977: 489-90).

In North Eastern Frontier Agency – (NEFA), Pandit Jawaharlal Nehru gave 'priority' to roads and schools and opined that – "given these communication and schools, they would advance rapidly and give a credit to the country in many ways" (1952-A).

Pandit Jawaharlal Nehru's love for the tribal communities found expression in his efforts to mix with them as frequently as possible, to show friendly and familiar gesture...and safeguard their interests (Vidyarthi 1968). Addressing an All India Conference of the tribal communities, held at Jagdalpur, in March 1955, he advised his tribal brethren in the following words:

"Wherever you live, you should live in your own way. This is what I want you to decide yourselves, how you would like to live. Your old customs and habits are good. We want that they should survive, but at the same time we want that you should be educated and should do your part in welfare of our country" (1955:16).

In spite of his anxiety to see the tribal communities educationally and economically advanced, he always hoped that there would be no attempt made to impose other ways of life on them in a hurry...."Let the change come gradually and be worked out by the tribal communities themselves" (Nehru 1957).

Observations, Analysis and Discussion

Literacy and level of education are two basic indicators of the level of development achieved by a group/society. The Literacy results in more awareness besides contributing to the overall improvement of health, hygiene and other social conditions.

Literacy and Educational Level – Among Scheduled Tribes in Maharashtra State

According to the 2001 census, the overall literacy rate among the tribal population in Maharashtra State is 55.20. This is less than the overall literacy rate 64.87, for the general population in Maharashtra State, during the 1991 census.

The literacy rate among the male population from the tribal population in Maharashtra, as per 2001 census is 68.42. This is less than the literacy rate 76.56, among the male population from the general population in Maharashtra State, during 1991 census.

The literacy rate among the female population from the tribal population in Maharashtra, as per 2001 Census is 43.10. This is less than the literacy rate 52.30, among the female population from the general population in Maharashtra State, during 1991 census.

This table indicates that the rate of literacy among the female population from the tribal population in Maharashtra is less than:

(i) the literacy rate of the male population from the tribal population in Maharashtra; and

(ii) the literacy rate of the female population from the general population in Maharashtra.

Table 3.1: Literacy among Scheduled Tribes

Literacy (Maharashtra State)						
Year	General Population			Tribal Population		
	Male	Female	Total	Male	Female	Total
1961	42.04	16.76	29.82	12.55	1.75	07.21
1971	51.04	26.43	39.13	19.06	4.21	11.74
1981	58.65	34.63	47.02	32.38	11.94	22.29
1991	76.56	52.30	64.87	49.08	24.08	36.77
2001	86.27	67.00	76.90	68.42	43.10	55.20

Source: Census of India 19961, 1971, 1981, 1991 and 2001.

A low rate of female literacy in India has always been a matter of concern. Female literacy in India can be attributed to several economic and social compulsions. (Mahatma Jotirao Phule a social reformer in Maharashtra did a pioneering work in the field of educating the girls and women from down-trodden classes of the society. He did this work with the help of his wife Savitribai, many years before getting independence. In the city of Pune, he started a school for girls, when the girls were not allowed to take education. Both Jotiba and Savitribai were harassed by the orthodox people in the society. In recognition of this pioneering work, the building in which the school for girls was located, has been declared to be preserved as a National Monument).

This Trend of Female Literacy Reflects Gender Inequality and Discrimination

Moreover, indicators of socio-economic development and the physical quality of life index in several sociological/ anthropological studies have clearly brought out the relevance of literacy and education of girls and women. The National Policy of Education (1986) has assigned an emphatic, interventionist role to educate the girls for bringing about changes in the status of women, leading to empowerment of women.

Once women perceive the relevance of education, they would willingly send their children, especially girls, to school.

If Women are Educated, then:

- child marriages would be prevented;
- they will have an awareness about maternal and child health;
- they will have knowledge and awareness about health and family welfare programmes;
- they will be prepared for acceptance of small family size norm;
- there will be a strong depressant effect on child bearing;
- they will have knowledge and awareness about health, hygiene and sanitation;

Table 3.2: Literacy in Maharashtra – Scheduled Tribes Population and General Population

Population	Literacy		
	Male	Female	Total
Scheduled Tribes	68.42	43.10	55.20
General Population	86.27	67.00	76.90

Source: Census of India 2001.

According to 2001 Census, percentage of literate persons (those who can read and write with understanding) aged 7 years and above, among ST population of Maharashtra is 55.2 per cent, which is lower than 76.9 per cent reported for the state population as a whole. The literacy data shows that the ST population of the state has made significant improvement in literacy during the decade 1991-2001. The literacy rate, which was 36.8 per cent in 1991, has increased by 18.4 percentage points in 2001. Though the literacy rate has improved substantially among ST population – 'it is still much below the literacy rate of the state population'. The female literacy rate of 43.1 per cent among ST population is lower as compared to 67.0 per cent among the total female population of the state.

Table 3.3: Educational Level Attained by Scheduled Tribes in Maharashtra

Educational Level	Percentage
- Literate without educational level	03.3
- Below Primary	41.7
- Primary	25.7
- Middle	13.6
- Secondary/Higher Secondary/Intermediate	13.4
- Technical and Non-technical Diploma	00.2
- Graduate and above	02.1

* *Source*: Census of India - 2001.

Out of the total literates, 45 per cent are literates without any educational level, or have attained educational level below Primary level. The literates, who have attained education up to Primary and Middle levels constitute 25.7 per cent and 13.6 per cent respectively. 13.4 per cent are having educational level up-to Secondary/Higher Secondary levels, implying that about every 7th Scheduled Tribe literate, is a Matriculate. The percentage of Literates with educational level up-to Graduation and above is 2.1.

The 'educational level' table shows that the drop-out is conspicuous at two levels:

(i) after the Primary level; and

(ii) after Secondary/Higher Secondary levels.

Among the Majority of the Scheduled Tribes

Literacy and Educational level reflect the Network of Schools and Enrolment.

[The state of Maharashtra has been witnessing the phenomena of non-tribal communities 'posing' as belonging to tribal communities – by virtue of partial/complete similarity in nomenclature. This phenomenon is reflected in the census data also. Hence, as far as the scheduled tribe population is concerned, the different demographic indices are inflated at least to a considerable extent (Gaikwad John S. 1986). This is true in case of the indices related to literacy also. Hence this fact needs to be kept in mind while considering the census data related to scheduled tribe population in Maharashtra]

Ashram Schools: Scenario in Maharashtra

Prior to 1972, there were a few Ashram schools in tribal areas of Maharashtra State. Most of these Ashram Schools were managed by Voluntary Organizations. During 1972, Government of India encouraged the State Governments to implement the ambitious scheme of Ashram School Complex in the Tribal Sub Plan areas in different states. Accordingly the Government of Maharashtra launched the scheme of Ashram School Complex in the State. To begin with, about 31 Ashram School Complex were established by the Government of Maharashtra during 1972-73. During 1972-73, there were about 20 Ashram schools managed by Voluntary/ Non-Government organizations. At present there are about 600 Government Ashram Schools in Maharashtra. In addition to the Ashram Schools managed by Government, there are about 600 Ashram Schools managed by voluntary/non-government organizations. As per the Government policy, the voluntary organizations get 100 per cent Salary grant, in addition to the grants required for the day to day needs of the resident students.

Apart from Ashram Schools, the tribal areas in Maharashtra also have Primary Schools (day Schools) managed by the Zilla Parishads.

Enrolment in Ashram Schools

Despite the growing network of Ashram Schools in the Tribal areas, and the increasing awareness about importance of education among the tribal communities, there are many children who are never enrolled in Ashram Schools or in the nearby Primary Schools (day Schools).

Enrolment in Government Ashram Schools is preferred the most because the admission makes the students eligible for free food and clothing, apart from free education. It is a fact that even if the parents are willing, some children do not get admission in standard I, in the Ashram Schools (managed either by Government or by a voluntary organization). It is also observed that the parents do not prefer to admit their children in the nearby Primary/day Schools.

It has been observed that the total number of female students enrolled is much less for all the classes (Bhanu and Kulkarni 1995). Further they observe that "only 50 per cent of the eligible children (6 to 14 years) attend the schools. There are a few villages where more than 80 per cent of the eligible children never attended the school" (1995:47).

Retention/Dropouts

Retention needs to be looked as an important index of success of the programme and not merely as "Education Wastage".

The following Table 3.4 illustrates the trend of average number of students enrolled in the Tribal Sub Plan Area in Maharashtra State.

Table 3.4: Average Number of Students Enrolled in Tribal Sub-plan Area in Maharashtra

Standard/Stage	Boys	Girls	Total
I	1,08,700	0,91,400	2,00,100
V	0,56,000	0,39,600	0,95,600
VIII	0,35,500	0,20,400	0,55,900
X	0,25,300	0,13,000	0,38,300

(Number of students rounded to nearest hundred).

Source: Table 8 – from 'Adiwasinche Shikshan' by Dr. Govind Gare.

It is observed that while the average enrolment in standard I in the Tribal Sub Plan Area in Maharashtra State is about 2 lakh children, the average number of students enrolled in standard VIII is about 55,000. This number further comes down to about 38,000 students at standard Xth level. Hence, it is observed that the enrolment decreases from standard I to standard X.

As far as the enrolment of girls is concerned, it is observed to be apparently in tune with the sex ratio, only during the enrolment in standard I. Thereafter the average number of enrolment for girls is observed to be declining rapidly. The enrolment of girls at standard X level is about 50 per cent of the enrolment of boys. (Gaikwad John S 1984, 1989).

Drop-out at an Early Stage

In a study regarding Ashram Schools, Ghode M. (1995) observes that – "the Ashram School children complained about the language used by their teachers, which was not easily grasped by them as it was different from their dialect". (1995:181).

One more factor which may be considered to be responsible for drop-outs at primary stage itself is the feeling of 'alienation' imposed by Marathi – as the medium of instruction. The dialects spoken by Bhil, Pawara, Korku, Kolam, Gond, Pardhi, Halba are entirely different from Marathi. Hence this situation demands that the teachers should feel comfortable to communicate with the students (at least in lower classes), in their own dialect.

Pandit Jawaharlal Nehru gave considerable thought on the language problem which he considered exceedingly important from the psychological point of view. He made it perfectly and absolutely clear that – "Government would encourage the tribal languages". He stood not only for allowing the tribal languages to continue but made it his policy "to encourage and help them to flourish" (Vidyarthi L. P. 1968). In this matter, he was greatly influenced by Lenin and others who won the goodwill of the tribal people of the Soviet Republic by encouraging their languages, by going out of their way in helping hundreds of dialects, by preparing dictionaries and vocabularies and even by evolving new scripts where there were none (Vidyarthi L. P. 1968).

Pandit Jawaharlal Nehru was convinced that it was a wise policy of Lenin of winning over illiteracy and above all to create an impression on them that they could live their own lives and in the light of this lesson, he advised all of us "to go out of our way to do so in context with Indian Tribal population" (1952).

The problem of medium of instruction has been posing a great irritant partly because we have not understood the tribal sentiment for their own dialects and partly because disintegrative Socio-Political forces misguide the tribal communities.

An UNESCO report on the medium of instruction, emphatically recommends that even where leaders of the tribal people do not want their language to be the medium of instruction, an attempt should be made to persuade them to change their mind. Article 350 A expects every local authority to provide adequate facilities for instruction in the mother-tongue at the primary stage (Ratha S. N. 1986).

Apart from the problem related to dialect, faced by the tribal students at an earlier stage, equally important is – the 'impact of the contents of the text books', at least at an earlier stage. The contents of the text books certainly play an important role in shaping the attitudes, outlook and interest of the children. Hence there is a need to consider this vital fact and design the text books for tribal children at least in lower classes. Text books containing familiar context is likely to have the potential of binding force that can prevent the dropout at an earlier stage.

Verrier Elwin (1963) observes that – in the successful formulation of the policy for the tribal education, text books assume great importance. They should include lessons depicting the life of tribal communities, their folklore, songs, history and the lives of their cultural heroes. These subjects should be woven into ordinary text books as well to enable the non-tribal and tribal people to understand each other and give them added confidence that their way of life, history and culture are getting adequate support from other members of the society.

Taking into consideration, the conditions and special needs of the tribal communities, the Dhebar Commission had suggested a separate cadre of teachers for tribal areas (quoted in Vidyarthi L. P. 1986).

Ghode M. (1995) further observes that recreational facilities are not available for the Ashram School children, during their leisure time. Further it can be stated that in case of young children, the feeling of home sickness, loneliness and shyness are yet another important factors which contribute to the phenomena of dropouts at an earlier stage. It is obvious that the small children would more frequently remember their home, parents and others in the new environment.

At this point it needs to be elaborated that the earlier Scheme of Ashram School Complex was more comprehensive. The educational programme and the hostel were considered to be a single unit. With the provision of teachers' quarters, teachers were always expected to be 'near' the students even after the school hours. The teachers in the Ashram Schools had an opportunity to play the role of parents of the students in Ashram Schools.

After facing many hurdles, all the activities other than formal education were completely discontinued. The educational programme and the hostel became independent of one another. The teachers are almost dissociated from the students, after the school hours. The Hotel Superintendent is expected to look after the School children after the School hours. However, the Hostel Superintendent concentrates only upon his/her responsibility of providing food to the Ashram School children.

Another major reason for drop-outs has been observed to be the responsibility of contribution in the income-generation activities or helping and supporting the family.

These Responsibilities Include:

- Participation in the agricultural activities.
- Participation in the operations in the forests.
- Participation in the activities related to food gathering.
- Participation in household activities.
- Looking after younger brothers/sisters.
- Cooking.

- Early marriage is an important factor responsible for drop-out of girls.

Regarding the apathy shown by the tribal communities for sending their children in schools – Elwin observes that – "For a tribal family, to send its grown up girl or boy to school is essentially a matter of economics; and entails dislocation in the traditional pattern of division of labour,.....many parents cannot just afford to send their children to school" (Elwin 1963:84).

Lack of motivation, enthusiasm and interest in studies, among some of the first generation learners, results in failure. This further leads to inferiority complex that ultimately leads to abandoning the stream of formal education. It is apparent that being first generation learners, many of the tribal children are not capable of adjusting themselves with the structured set up of formal education.

The author had an opportunity to interview drop-out students and their parents in the tribal areas of Nandurbar, Nashik, Gadchiroli, Thane and Amravati Districts. Some of the parents indicated the awareness that if their children are educated they can get jobs. Despite such awareness, they were not at all keen to educate their children. Some of the illiterate parents indicated that – "educated children are a loss to the family".

This feeling is deep-rooted in their experience that – after exposure to the mainstream of formal education, many individuals partially dissociate themselves from the traditions of the community. Some individuals develop 'disliking' for activities related to agriculture. These 'disliking' results in an avoidance of activities related to agriculture. In such cases the activities related to agriculture are considered to be below dignity. Such individuals aspire for white-collared jobs in Government offices. In the quest for a Government job, some of them make a compromise with the situation and are satisfied to accept even class IV jobs.

Thus it is observed that ignorance, illiteracy and lack of awareness, motivation and enthusiasm lead to apathy for education. The tribal parents do not understand the relevance and importance of education. They are not aware that education has the potential to change the future of their children. Hence they do not feel like compromising with their problematic situation and motivate their children to complete their education properly. Though the comprehensive package of free education along with free food and clothing is apparently attractive, it is a fact that this package does not have the potential binding force, which can prevent the drop-outs.

It is observed that the drop-out rate among the day scholars is considerably higher in comparison to the drop out rate among the students in the Ashram Schools. It is a fact that if the parents are educated, then they themselves try their level best to prevent their children from getting off the tract of formal education.

While doing research on Tribal Health, the author observed that the tribal communities consider the entire Health Care Services set up and Health Programmes as – 'something imposed from outside world' (Gaikwad John S. 1995). It is apparent that the pre-literate tribal communities look at the formal education system as – 'something imposed from outside world, which is not relevant and important in the frame work of their traditional culture'.

Conclusion and Epilogue

Considering the network of about 1200 Ashram Schools in the Tribal Sub Plan areas of Maharashtra State, there is a need to ponder upon how best this network of Ashram Schools can be utilised to improve the quality of education. The network of Ashram Schools should become effective, efficient and yield optimum results in term of academic excellence and quality. Apart from the present network, there is a need to establish more Ashram Schools. Moreover attaining these objectives and goals is not dependant merely upon availability of funds and infrastructure.

In order to achieve these goals, there is a need of a judicious combination of political will, effective administration, academic aptitude, rationality, efficiency, motivation, zeal, dedication, sincerity etc., on the part of the administrators and teachers. (Gaikwad John and Gare G. M. 1986). Moreover, psychological approach is necessary for a result oriented outcome.

The illiterate and semi-literate tribal communities need to be made aware about the importance and relevance of educating their children. Their apathy needs to be replaced with enthusiasm for education of their children.

Apart from academic excellence and quality, there is a need to tackle the problem of drop-outs. The students should become aware about the need, relevance and importance of formal education for their development. Such an awareness and enthusiasm would change their attitude and outlook that will motivate them to remain in the mainstream of formal education. The first generation learners need to be equipped with the techniques of adapting and adjusting to the new environment of formal education.

Special efforts are necessary to prevent the girls from going away from the main stream of formal education. The parents and the girls both need to be aware that in a changing scenario, new employment opportunities for girls are opening up in all fields. The National policy of Education (1986), has assigned an emphatic interventionist role to educate girls for bringing about changes in the Status of women, leading to empowerment of women. Empowerment of Tribal Women would certainly contribute to increase in literacy and educational level, along with associated developments.

Further this would facilitate an overall 'sustainable development' which would ultimately contribute to the 'empowerment' and an improvement of 'quality of life' of tribal communities.

REFERENCES

Bhanu and Kulkarni (1995), Drop-outs in a Tribal Context. In – An overview of Tribal Research Studies. Ed. By Dr. Navinchandra Jain and Dr. Robin D. Tribhuwan. Tribal Research and Training Institute, M. S., Pune.

Census of India (1961), Registrar General of India, New Delhi.

Census of India (1971), Registrar General of India, New Delhi.

Census of India (1981), Registrar General of India, New Delhi.

Census of India (1991), Registrar General of India, New Delhi.

Census of India (2001), Registrar General of India, New Delhi.

Elwin Verrier (ed) (1963), A New Deal for Tribal India. Ministry of Home Affairs, Government of India, New Delhi.

Gaikwad John S. (1984), 'Adiwasi Striya ani Shikshan' (in Marathi). Hakara Vol. 5, No. 3, July – Septemnber 1984. Maharashtra Association for Anthropological Sciences, Pune.

Gaikwad John S. (1986), 'Adiwasi Vikasat Shikshanachi Navin Disha, Navin Avhane'. Tribal Research Bulletin Vol. VIII, No. 2, March 1986. Tribal Research and Training Institute, M.S., Pune.

Gaikwad John S. (1986), A Demographic Profile of Tribal in Maharashtra State.

Gaikwad John S. (1986), Tribal Research and Training Institute, M. S., Pune.

Gaikwad John S. (1986), Tribal Research Bulletin, Vol. IX. No. 1, September 1986.

Gaikwad John S. (1989), Tribal Research and Training Institute, M. S., Pune.

Gaikwad John S. (1989), Tribal Research Bulletin, Vol. XI, No. 2, September 1989.

Gaikwad John S. (1995), Cultural Profile of Health in a Tribal Community. Ph.D. Thesis Submitted to the University of Pune.

Gaikwad John S. (1989), 'Adiwasi Upayojana Kshetrateel Adiwasi Streeyanche Shikshan' (in Marathi).

Gare Govind M. (2007), Adiwasinche Shikshan. Saket Prakashan, Pune.

Ghode Mangal (1995), Status of Ashram Schools in Maharashtra State. In – An Overview of Tribal Research Studies. Ed. By Dr. Navinchandra Jain and Dr. Robin D. Tribhuwan. Tribal Research and Training Institute, M.S., Pune.

Mathur H. M. (ed) (1977), A New Deal for Tribal India (Pages 489-90). In – Anthropology in the Development Process. Ed. By Mathur Hari Mohan. Vikas Publishing House Pvt. Ltd., New Delhi.

Ministry of Human Resource Development (1986), New Education Policy, Ministry of Human Resource Development, Government of India, New Delhi.

National-Literacy Mission (1992), 'Women and Literacy'. In – Literacy: A Peoples Movement. Directorate of Adult Education, National Literacy Mission, Government of India, New Delhi.

Nehru Jawaharlal (1952), A Speech on Return from a Tour of NEFA.

Nehru Jawaharlal (1952), Inaugural Speech at the Conference for Tribes and Tribal (Scheduled) Areas held at New Delhi. Vanyajati, Vol. XII, July 1964, No. 3, New Delhi.

Nehru Jawaharlal (1955), Inaugural Address at the Conference for Tribes and Tribal (Scheduled) Areas, held at Jagdalpur. Published in the Report of Bharatiya Adimjati Sevak Sangh, New Delhi.

Nehru Jawaharlal (1957), 'Foreword' to the First Edition to Verrier Elwin's – A Philosophy for NEFA, Shillong, NEFA.

Nehru Jawaharlal (1959), 'Foreword' to the Second Edition to Verrier Elwin's – A Philosophy for NEFA, Shillong, NEFA.

Ratha S. N. (1986), A Note on Tribal Education . In – Tribal Development and its Administration. Ed. By Dr. L. P. Vidyarthi. Concept Publishing Company, New Delhi.

Vidyarthi L. P. (ed.) (1968), Nehru's Approach to Tribal Cultures. In – Applied Anthropology in India. Ed. by Dr. L. P. Vidyarthi, Kitab Mahal, Allahabad.

4

Educational Facilities and School Drop-out in Tribal Areas
A District Level Analysis in Andhra Pradesh

1. Dr. Murali Vallapureddy

ABSTRACTS

The present paper is an analysis of school drop-out in Tribal Areas in Andhra Pradesh based on both primary and secondary data at district level. Developing a very good infrastructure is a prerequisite of a good schooling system which will be make more attractive to students and help in increasing the enrolment in schools as well as improving the quality of education. The improvement in the economic status of poor families is the pre-condition far stopping drop-outs in school. In the short run, the government may consider the policy option of enrolling all the children of poor families in the residential schools compulsorily. These residential schools should be run on professional excellence.

Keywords: School Drop-out, School Enrolment.

1. Associate Professor, Mahboobia Panjetan PG College, Warangal, India. Mobile +91-9441271943. E-mail: dr.vmreddy@yahoo.co.in

Introduction

Education is a key to sustainable development. For peace and stability within and among countries, and effective participation in the economy of the 21st century education is an indispensable means for which is witnessing rapid globalisation. While traditionally 'Education' has meant children in schools, it is equally important to address the learning needs of adults. Combining these two components of the learning continuum, most countries around the world have enlarged the scope of educational planning to include basic education and adult literacy under the rubric of 'Education for All'.

As per the article 21A and 93rd Constitutional Amendments 2009, education has become a fundamental right. This article clearly spells out the responsibility of the state to the extent of providing free and compulsory education to all the children from the age of 6 to 14 years. Government is committed to achieve total literacy by 2015 and in this direction initiated several schemes for both quantitative and qualitative improvement.

Education has a pivotal role to guide and induce the person to the process of self-realisation. An educated person carries autonomous and authentic ideas and not one who has been conditioned or indoctrinated. Education is direction but in a fashion that does not estrange or alienate one self but puts one on to the path of meaningful learning and realising.

For educated person we make a positive value judgment. There is an expectation that education will improve the qualities of life of a person and will behave in a better manner than one who is not educated. There is a sense of being let down, disappointment and dismay if an educated person can not conduct himself in a manner that is rational, morally good and socially responsible. It is clear that by education is meant all-round development of a person, not merely specialisation or professional training. Educationists too stress that education is a holistic process and not only a training of the intellect. It is development of moral, social, aesthetic as well as rational capacity. People might differ on the degree of importance that they place on these various dimensions but most would include all these in their notion of an educated person.

Educational facilities definitely promote the prosperity of the society and contribute positively to gross domestic product and create employment opportunity. It has a positive effect on reduction of poverty, population growth, crime rate and better health condition.

The knowledge possessed by the population and their capacity and training to use it effectively is also very important. Expenditure on education, training and research can contribute to the productivity by raising the quality of the workforce, and these outlays yield a counting return in the future. If this expenditure is considered as expenditure on capital then the proportion of capital formation in national income in the rich countries would be much higher. But since poor countries do not make huge investments in the formation of human capital, this broad interpretation of capital would not increase significantly in proportion to their national income spent on capital formation.

While investment on human resources has been witnessing a high growth in advanced countries, the negligible amount of human investment in under developed countries has done little to extend the capacity of the people to meet the challenges of accelerated development. The characteristic of 'economic backwardness' is still manifest in several ways like low labour efficiency, factor immobility, limited specialisation in occupations and in trade, a deficient supply of entrepreneurship, and customary values and traditional social institutions that minimize the incentives for economic change. It has to be recognised that the wrong kind of education unaccompanied by the required complementary actions can check or reverse the process of development.

To mitigating the contemporary problems of developing countries particularly in India, for the efficient utilisation of human resources, education continues to be a neglected part of planning of India. To attract the down trodden such as SCs/STs, minorities communities and women, it is essential to allocate more funds for the establishment, expansion and strengthening of educational facilities like appointment of teachers, infrastructure, equipment, drinking water, sanitation, compound wall, play ground, library etc., which are available to the rural masses. The existing edge of challenge is in rural schools. More than a century ago, Jyothi Rao Phule wrote in his moving appeal to the hunter commission (1984) that conditions in rural schools were terrible.

Government of India quantitatively forced a target of investing 6 per cent of national income on education on the recommendation of the Education Commission (1966) and the Kothari Commission also suggested that a higher (more than 6%) investment would need to be allocated on education in India (1986). But the goal remains elusive even today. This is one of the glaring promises that continue to remain a goal repeatedly postponed, unfulfilled and often reiterated. The present UPA Government in its Common Minimum Programme (CMP) has laid greatest emphasis on the development of social sectors to achieve a higher economic growth along with social justice and particularly decided to incur more on education and it has to be done in a phased manner".

The proportion of GNP invested on education in many other developing countries including India are very low as compared to other developed countries of the world. According to Human Development Report, 2004, India's was ranks 78th out of 137 countries. India was spending 4.1 per cent of her GNP on education (1999-2001). In comparison, a large number of countries spend more than 6-8 per cent and some of them even more than 10 per cent on education. Expenditure on education influencing literacy levels (Sharif and Ghosh 2000). The share of elementary education in the total expenditure on education continues to be below 50 per cent as against the required 65-70 per cent to achieve universal literacy.

Literacy Rates in India 1951-2011

In order to fulfill the constitutional obligation, India has lunched the programme of Sarva Shiksha Abhiyam to achieve Universalisation of Elementary Education in the country by the year 2010. It implies that all children in the age group 6 to below 14 years get enrolled in a regular school or an alternative school system and they do not drop out from school before completing the full cycle of elementary education. Efforts are being made on various fronts to ensure that no child in this age group remains out of school. The programme is an effort towards recognition of the need for improving the performance of the school system through a community owned approach and ensuring quality elementary education in a mission mode to all children which also seeks to bridge gender and social gaps.

Table 4.1: Literacy Rates in India 1951-2011

Census Year	Persons	Male	Females	Male - Female Gap in Literacy Rate
1951	18.33	27.16	8.66	18.50
1961	28.30	40.40	15.35	25.05
1971	34.45	45.96	21.97	23.98
1981	43.57	56.38	29.76	26.62
1991	52.21	64.13	39.29	24.84
2001	65.38	75.26	54.16	21.70
2011	74.04	82.14	65.46	16.68

Source: Provisional data of the 2011 census.

The15th official census in India was calculated in the year 2011. In a country like India, literacy is the main foundation for social and economic growth. When the British rule ended in India in the year 1947 the literacy rate was just 12 per cent. Over the years, India has changed socially, economically, and globally. After the 2011 census, literacy rate India 2011 was found to be 74.04 per cent. Compared to the adult literacy rate here the youth literacy rate is about 9 per cent higher. Though this seems like a very great accomplishment, it is still a matter of concern that still so many people in India cannot even read and write. The numbers of children who do not get education especially in the rural areas are still high. Though the government has made a law that every child under the age of 14 should get free education, the problem of illiteracy is still at large.

It is clear from Table 4.1 that from 1951 census to 2011 census the literacy rates have shown a substantial improvement. The literacy rate which was only 18.33 per cent in 1951 rose to 52.21 per cent in 1991 and further increased to 74.04.4 per cent in 2011. According to the Census of India, 2011 the literacy rate has gone up to 82.14 per cent for male and 65.46 per cent for females. Interestingly, literacy rate improved sharply among females as compared to males. While the effective literacy rate for males rose from 75.26 to 82.14 per cent marking a rise of 6.9 per cent, it increased by 11.8 per cent for females to go from 53.67 to 65.46 per cent.

Educational Status of Andhra Pradesh

During 2011-12, the department provides schooling facility to school age population of 1.29 crore children. Out of which 52.76 lakhs were in Primary School, 21.57 lakhs were in Upper Primary School and 54.04 lakhs were in High School. Out of 1,02,436 schools in Andhra Pradesh, in the Elementary Education sector there were 66,721 Primary Schools and 15,759 Upper Primary Schools. Under Secondary Education there were 19,770 High Schools and 186 Higher Secondary Schools. Out of 1,02,436 schools, 114 were Central Government, 7,716 State Government, 66,393 MP/ZP, 2,115 Municipal, 3,335 Pvt. Aidedand 22,763 Pvt. Unaided.

Teachers

During 2011-12, there were 4,95,138 teachers in position in all types of schools in the state. Out of which, 1,89,722 in primary schools, 97,015 in upper primary schools, 2,04,060 in High schools and 4,314 teachers in higher secondary schools.

Table 4.2: Educational Facilities

Year	Primary Schools			Upper Primary Schools			High Schools			Higher Scondary Schools		
	Sc.	En.	Teac.	Sc.	En.	Teac.	Sc.	En.	Teac.	Sc.	En.	Teac.
1	2	3	4	5	6	7	8	9	10	11	12	13
1996-97	48899	5635379	106974	7733	2130398	50287	8178	3505246	107506	93	99848	4365
1997-98	49919	5936750	121446	8142	2274897	58509	8566	3617222	112850	95	96131	4387
1998-99	51836	6237735	136363	8713	2443179	62845	8897	3767758	115670	97	101850	4654
1999-00	55398	6373837	136853	9530	2614524	69117	9659	4177431	122891	88	92292	4154
2000-01	55901	6060394	133546	9804	2628185	69265	10277	4537791	131324	82	82227	3847
2001-02	58249	5230748	127313	14472	3322826	85263	11464	4963392	145246	73	74765	3498
2002-03	63362	6351072	173731	15110	3389189	102152	12570	4078358	140019	79	78336	3628
2003-04	63897	5967010	172601	15215	3149964	100365	13160	4330479	140826	82	82033	3305
2004-05	61680	5524363	166935	16667	3172877	103985	14342	4633242	140399	79	80586	3475
2005-06	62159	5398008	166790	17290	3172134	106215	15437	4839243	142544	98	102538	3958
2006-07	62162	5513155	167723	17823	3246096	112388	16195	4988791	153988	97	103188	4056
2007-08	62464	5366949	167059	17957	3110686	110949	16937	5114442	156887	99	99664	4241
2008-09	65609	5686045	183197	14942	2492198	94662	17376	5369962	167159	100	110955	4127
2009-10	65932	5392253	169159	15384	2395849	90077	18143	5477427	187709	104	100827	4147
2010-11	66834	5463896	174069	15421	2329730	93003	18776	5397690	205179	173	126870	4304
2011-12	66721	5276876	189722	15759	2157321	97015	19770	5407778	204060	186	138863	4314

Source: School Education Department, *Note*: Sc= No. of Schools; En. No = Enrolment; Teac. = Teachers.

Government have committed itself to fill-up all the existing teacher vacancies and sanction necessary additional posts to achieve teacher pupil ratio of 1: 40. The percentage pass of students in S.S.C examinations during 2009-10 is 81.63 which is higher than the previous year pass of 78.83 per cent. (Table 4.2)

A person, who is 7 years and above and who is able to read and write with understanding in any one language is considered as Literate. The literacy rate of the state is 67.66 in 2011 as against 44.08 in 1991. The literacy rate of the state is lower than that of all India literacy rate at 74.04. Among the districts, Hyderabad is at the top with 80.96. The least literate district is Mahabubnagar with 56.06 per cent. Male literacy rate is 75.56 as against that of female at 59.74. District-wise literacy rate is given in Table 4.3. (*See table on next page*)

The Directorate of School Education deals with School Education catering to the educational needs of children. The pattern of School Education in Andhra Pradesh is 5+2+3 *i.e.* 5 years of Primary Education, 2 years of Upper Primary Education and 3 years of Secondary Education.

Government of Andhra Pradesh intends to achieve the goal of universalisation of elementary education by recognising education as a potential instrument for Human Development. The primary goal of the state is to increase steadily the overall literacy levels. Provision of schooling facilities within a distance of 1 km., of all rural habitations is a pre-requisite for achieving universal access. For this, Primary Schools are started in almost all places within a distance of 1 km.

Teacher-Pupil Ratio

A major element of the approach to strengthening education will be to improve current learning levels by lowering the teacher pupil ratio. Government has already committed to fill-up all the existing teacher vacancies and sanctioning the additional posts necessary to achieve teacher-pupil ratio of 1:40. The Teacher Pupil Ratios for Primary, Upper Primary and High Schools are shown in Table 4.4. *(See table on page 48)*

Table 4.3: Literacy Rates by Sex for State and Districts

Sl. No.	District	Males			Females			Total		
		1991	2001	2011	1991	2001	2011	1991	2001	2011
1	2	3	4	5	6	7	8	9	10	11
1.	Adilabad	45.05	64.98	71.22	20.60	40.30	51.99	32.96	52.68	61.55
2.	Nizamabad	47.33	64.91	72.66	21.35	39.48	52.33	34.18	52.02	62.25
3.	Karimnagar	50.79	67.09	74.72	23.37	42.75	55.18	37.17	54.90	64.87
4.	Medak	45.15	64.33	72.50	19.25	38.66	52.49	32.41	51.65	62.53
5.	Hyderabad	78.90	83.74	83.35	63.56	73.50	78.42	71.52	78.80	80.96
6.	Ranga Reddy	60.43	75.26	84.00	36.91	56.49	71.82	49.07	66.16	78.05
7.	Mahabubnagar	40.80	56.63	66.27	18.03	31.89	45.65	29.58	44.41	56.06
8.	Nalgonda	50.53	69.23	74.94	24.92	44.68	55.05	38.00	57.15	65.05
9.	Warangal	51.98	68.88	75.91	26.08	45.09	56.45	39.30	57.13	66.16
10.	Khammam	50.04	66.11	73.20	30.53	47.44	57.85	40.50	56.89	65.46
11.	Srikakulam	49.14	67.19	72.25	23.52	43.68	52.56	36.22	55.31	62.30
12.	Vizianagaram	45.93	62.37	69.04	22.47	39.91	50.16	34.19	51.07	59.49
13.	Visakhapatnam	56.13	69.68	75.48	34.60	50.12	60.00	45.51	59.96	67.70

Contd...

1	2	3	4	5	6	7	8	9	10	11
14.	East Godavari	55.32	70.00	74.91	42.26	60.94	67.82	48.79	65.48	71.35
15.	West Godavari	59.75	78.05	77.63	46.98	68.99	71.05	53.38	73.53	74.32
16.	Krishna	60.55	74.39	79.13	45.54	63.19	69.62	53.16	68.85	74.37
17.	Guntur	56.54	71.24	75.40	35.85	53.74	60.64	46.35	62.54	67.99
18.	Prakasam	53.14	69.35	73.54	27.06	45.08	53.40	40.30	57.38	63.53
19	Nellore	58.04	73.67	75.93	36.99	56.38	62.30	47.61	65.08	69.15
20.	Kadapa (Y. S. R)	63.14	75.83	78.41	32.35	49.54	57.26	48.12	62.83	67.88
21.	Kurnool	53.24	65.96	71.36	26.04	40.03	50.81	39.97	53.22	61.13
22.	Anantapur	55.92	68.38	74.09	27.61	43.34	54.31	42.18	56.13	64.28
23.	Chittoor	62.61	77.62	81.15	36.44	55.78	63.65	49.75	66.77	72.36
	Andhra Pradesh	**55.12**	**70.32**	**75.56**	**32.72**	**50.43**	**59.74**	**44.08**	**60.47**	**67.66**

Source: Census of India, 2001, Director of Census Operations, Andhra Pradesh and Census of India 2011 (provisional figures).

Table 4.4: Teacher Pupil Ratios

Year	Primary	Upper Primary	High School
2000-01	45	38	34
2001-02	41	39	34
2002-03	37	33	29
2003-04	35	31	31
2004-05	29	25	30
2005-06	28	25	30
2006-07	29	24	29
2007-08	28	23	28
2008-09	27	22	29
2009-10	28	23	28

Source: School Education Department.

Drop-out Rates

Drop-out rate is defined as a percentage of the number of children to total enrolment dropping out of the educational system in a particular year. The ratio does not take into account repeaters and children who enter the system after class-I. It is expected that every child who enters class-1 completes class-VII without discontinuing the school in between. With this view, efforts are being made to tackle the problem of drop-outs with the support of School Management Committees. The Drop-out Rate during 2011-12 in Primary Stage (Classes I-V) is 15.60, in Upper Primary Stage (Classes I-VII) is 20.79 and in Secondary Schools is 45.71. Details of Drop-out rates are shown in Table 4.5.

New Education Policy Perspectives in Andhra Pradesh

Enrolment

Steps are being taken to enroll all out of school children and to free the children working in the domestic sector and other organizations. As a result of the enrolment drive with the name of 'Badi Bata' from 1st - 16th June 2006 to enroll all school age children, as many as 14.41 Lakh children (5+)

Table 4.5: Drop-out Rates

Year	I – V			I - VII			I - X		
	Boys	Girls	Total	Boys	Girls	Total	Boys	Girls	Total
1971-72	69.34	72.53	70.65	77.80	86.91	81.59	87.62	94.37	90.56
1981-82	58.48	62.87	60.31	64.40	73.19	67.98	78.28	85.91	81.35
1991-92	52.15	57.04	54.28	61.17	69.17	64.65	72.76	79.31	75.54
2001-02	35.36	33.64	34.54	51.98	55.77	53.78	71.62	73.28	72.37
2003-04	42.42	42.80	42.61	52.71	55.92	54.27	65.28	68.53	66.70
2004-05	31.77	32.14	31.95	51.96	54.46	53.17	62.30	65.24	63.69
2005-06	24.61	24.85	24.73	50.26	52.37	51.30	62.24	65.20	63.67
2006-07	26.76	27.32	27.04	42.14	44.32	43.22	62.99	65.33	64.13
2007-08	19.10	18.48	18.79	33.26	35.23	34.24	62.30	64.00	63.13
2008-09	16.14	15.15	15.65	34.39	35.41	34.89	60.12	61.38	60.73
2009-10	16.34	15.24	15.80	26.38	26.50	26.44	52.73	54.2	53.36
2010-11	18.10	16.73	17.43	22.56	22.11	22.34	45.83	46.59	46.21
2011-12	15.93	15.27	15.60	21.51	20.06	20.79	45.43	45.99	45.71

Source: School Education Department.

enrolled into class-I. 1.64 Lakhs of out of school children were enrolled into regular/bridge schools. 522 Residential bridge courses and 3,063 Alternative and Innovative Education (AIE) centres have taken in 1.341 Lakh of children. Innovative strategies and interventions of the Government resulted in considerable increase in enrolment and retention. The strategy for achieving universal participation involves strengthening of the existing infrastructure, opening new primary schools, establishment of alternative schools and other types of educational facilities in smaller and unserved habitations. Due to these interventions and several other programmes, enrolment has increased significantly in all stages of education. Total enrolment as on 2011-12 was 129.81 lakhs in schools, out of which 52.77 lakhs (40.65%) were in Primary Schools, 21.58 lakhs (16.63%) and 54.08 lakhs (41.66%) were in Upper Primary and High Schools respectively and remaining Higher Secondary Schools.

Mid-Day Meal Programme

In order to bring back the children into schools and retain them in schools for achieving the objective of Education for All and to provide nutritious food to the children, for their physical and mental development, Midday Meal scheme (MDM) is being implemented from January 2003 in the state. Under the scheme, a minimum content of 450 calories and 12 grams of protein content is provided per child on each working day of the school for classes I to V and 700 calories and 20 grams of protein content is provided per child on each working day of the school for classes VI to X. Primary School, Upper Primary and High School Children of Classes I-X studying in Government/Local bodies and Aided institutions are covered under this scheme. Under the Mid-Day Meal programme, an amount of Rs. 597.29 crores, has been spent during 2007-08 to 2010-11 (Till Dec. 2011). The amounts include the state contribution besides the Central allocation. Under the scheme, 60.33 lakh students during 2007-08, 70.44 lakh students during 2008-09, 70.43 lakh students during 2009-10 and 74.44 lakhs students during 2010-11 have been covered. Government of

India is providing rice free of cost @ 100 grams per child per working day. Conversion cost is paid to the identified implementing agencies towards cooking cost.

Sarva Shiksha Abhiyan

Sarva Shiksha Abhiyan (SSA) is a comprehensive and integrated flagship programme of Government of India, to attain Universal Elementary Education (UEE) in the country in a mission mode. Launched in partnership with the State Governments and local self-governments, SSA aims to provide useful and relevant education to all the children in the 6-14 age groups by 2010. Under the SSA programme, an amount of Rs. 3134.68 crores was spent during the last four years 2007-08 to 2010-11 (Till Dec. 2011). Under this scheme, during the 4 year period, 210 new school buildings have been constructed, 170 schools have been made operational. Further, several schools have been provided with adequate drinking water facility and toilet facility. Due to the 221 infrastructure facilities and academic support, there has been improvement in enrolment as well as reducing drop out ratios.

Community Participation (School Management Committee)

For the first time in the country, Government of Andhra Pradesh has enacted 'Community Participation Act 1998' involving the community in school management. Resources are transferred to School Committees empowering them to plan, manage and promote quality education. In terms of 73rd and 74th Constitutional Amendments, Sarpanches/Ward Councilors have been made the Chairpersons of the School Management Committees.

Vidya Volunteers

In view of the large number of representations received from School Management Committees seeking Government support to achieve Universalisation of Primary Education and duly taking into account the inadequate teacher pupil ratio, Government of Andhra Pradesh decided to support School Management Committees to provide 'Vidya Volunteers'. Government decided to provide financial assistance on purely temporarily basis to School Management Committees to enlist Vidya Volunteers by them on contract basis. To improve the teacher pupil ratio in Primary Schools, Subject teachers in Upper Primary and High Schools for imparting the quality of education, 59,014 Vidya Volunteers were engaged during 2005-06 with an amount of Rs. 263.13 Lakhs.

Education for Minorities

Government of Andhra Pradesh is committed to the advancement and upliftment of Minorities in the state. With a view to promote Urdu Language in the state, 300 Urdu Teacher Posts were created additionally during 1997-98 are being continued every year. An amount of Rs. 291.02 Lakhs is provided during 2006-07. Government is granting de-reservation in respect of Urdu Medium Posts year after year. Vacancies, which could not be filled in due to non-availability, carried forward for selection.

District Institute of Education and Training (DIET)

Government of Andhra Pradesh has upgraded 23 Teacher Training Institutes as District Institute of Education and Training and one Tribal Teachers Training Institute at Utnoor as Sub-DIET in a phased manner. In 13 DIETs, Urdu medium parallel sections are functioning and 65 lecturer posts have been sanctioned. The Tamil medium parallel section with intake of 50 is functioning at DIET, Chittoor at Karvetinagar.

Improvement of Enrolment through Various Programmes

The Computer Education Programme is being implemented under BOOT Model by seven agencies in 5,000 High schools from 2008-09 for 5 years and in 1,300 high schools from 2010-11 for 5 years.

Tribal Education

The tribal population of Andhra Pradesh according to 2001 Census is 50.24 lakhs constituting about 6.59 per cent of the total population. Tribal Welfare Department is maintaining 599 Ashram Schools with a strength of 1,41,971, 442 Hostels with a strength of 77,420 and 4,317 Girijana Vidya Vikasa Kendras (Single Teacher Schools) renamed as Government

Primary Schools (TW) with a strength of 1,01,852. 81 per cent of students passed SSC exams held in March, 2010. 272 institutions are being run by Gurukulam (APTWREIS). 93 per cent of students in TW Residential Schools passed in SSC Public Examinations held in March, 2010. The lands recognised under RoFR Act are proposed to be developed under 'RoFR Land Development programme of MGNREGS' thus providing wage employment to poor tribal farmers as well as giving them an opportunity to develop their own lands. In the first phase, 1.6 lakh acres are proposed to be fully developed at an estimated cost of Rs. 310.00 cr. Under Recognition of Forest Rights Act, 2006 (RoFR) a total of 3,30,143 claims were received to cover 19,65,741 acres, and 1,67,582 certificates of titles were issued to cover 14,44,049 acres so far.

The Scheduled areas extend over 31,485.34 sq kms., which is about 11 per cent of total area of the State with 5,938 villages distributed in Srikakulam, Vizianagaram, Visakhapatnam, East Godavari, West Godavari, Khammam, Warangal, Adilabad and Mahabubnagar districts. There are no scheduled areas in other districts. There are 35 ST communities living in the State. Of the 50.24 lakhs tribal population, 30.47 lakhs are found in the above mentioned 9 districts. The remaining tribal population of 19.77 lakhs is distributed in the other districts. Areas inhabited by primitive tribal groups and remote areas of the ITDAs and MADAs are by and large lacking in necessary infrastructural facilities required for a minimum standard of living. The availability of infrastructure facilities in the tribal areas is far below the State and National averages.

The General Literacy rate is 60.5 as per 2001 Census, while the ST literacy is 37.04. Tribal Welfare Department was established in 1962 with an objective to assist the tribal population in the field of education, economic development and other programmes. Tribal development did not get translated into a definite programme of action till the 4th Plan period until the socio-economic development of STs was accepted as a general goal. The concept of tribal sub-plan strategy was evolved after a detailed comprehensive review of the tribal problem was taken during V Five-year Plan. For implementation of the strategy, Integrated Tribal Development Agencies (ITDAs) were conceived. During VI Five-year Plan, Modified Area Development Approach (MADA) was adopted to cover smaller areas of tribal concentration and for still smaller areas the cluster approach was adopted. Now there are 41 MADA Pockets and 17 Clusters. During VII Five-year Plan the programmes were extended to Dispersed Tribal Groups (DTGs) also.

By the end of IX Plan, the Programme priorities of Tribal Welfare Department are provision of incentives to students by way of free boarding and lodging for hostellers and package of incentives like supply of text books, note books, dresses etc. For the first time, 82 Primary Health Centres were sanctioned during 2004 exclusively for tribal areas to improve access to primary health care. All efforts are being made to ensure that all the tribal habitations are provided with safe drinking water. Government accorded high priority for the accelerated development of tribals by implementing socio-economic development programmes. Major focus is on Education, Health and Land based schemes.

Significance of the Study

In Andhra Pradesh introduced many programmes like Sarva Shiksha Abhiyan, Mid-day Meal programme, Community Participation, Vidhya Volunteers etc., to improvement of enroll all out of school children and to free the children working in the domestic sector and other organizations. To provide minimum basic facilities to schools such as construction of school building, providing accommodation, furniture, library and lab equipment etc., various schemes have been taken up. In spite of the government taking up these various activities the drop out rate has not reduced as per expectations. This studies aspects in Warangal district of Andhra Pradesh.

Methodology

The data for this study were collected from both primary and secondary sources. Primary data were collected for studying causes for drop-outs. The secondary data consists of enrollment of students in the district statistics records; causes for drop-outs have been analysed by direct interview method with coverage of 78 respondents *i.e.*, teachers, parents and students of Warangal district of Telangana region in Andhra Pradesh, India.

Objectives

- To study the educational facilities available in the sample area.
- To explore the accessibility of educational facilities to Schedule Tribes and women population.
- To find out the problems in getting proper educational services in government and private schools.
- To examine reasons for the drop-outs in the study area.
- To suggest some policy measures to achieve the targeted literacy levels in rural areas.

Profile of the Study Area

Warangal, which is one of the ten districts in the Telangana Region of Andhra Pradesh, is considered next to Hyderabad with economic, social education importance. There is a historical significance for Warangal town, served as the seat of power of the Yadava kings in the 8th Century AD and Kakatiya rulers from the 12th century AD onwards. Warangal then came under the influence of first of the Qutubshahi dynasty of Golkonda and then the Nizam of Hyderabad. While the resurgence of Warangal can be traced to the beginning of the 'Modern Age', the last decade has witnessed rapid acceleration of economic growth. (*See table 4.6 on next page*)

Boundaries

The district lies between the latitude of 17-19^{0} and 18-36^{0} north and longitudes of 78-49^{0} and 80-49^{0} east, and is above midsea level by 870ft - 1700ft. it is bounded on the north by Karimnagar district. On the west by Medak district, on the south by Nalgonda district and by Khammam district on the east and south-east. The geographical area of the district is

Table 4.6: Demographic Particulars of the Warangal District

S. No.	Category	Population
1.	Total population	3,522,644
2.	Density of population	274 persons per Sq. Km.
3.	Rural population	71.66%
4.	Urban population	28.34%
5.	Male population	17,66,257
6.	Female population	17,56,387
7.	Decadal growth rate of population	8.52 per cent
8.	Literate population	21,16,037
9.	Male literacy rate	12,11,953
10.	Female literacy rate	9,04,084
11.	ST population (2001 census)	4,57,679 (14.10%)

Source: Census of India 2011 (provisional figures).

12,846 sq. kms. The district possessed interesting pictures of geographical formations and contains minerals of economic importance. The soils of the district comprise of sandy loam's with parches of shallow black cotton soils, and at places even medium and deep black cotton soil.

Women self-help group movements have made indelible impact on district development in the shape of the promotion of literacy of women, decrease of population growth rate part of from empowering women economically and socially. Today there are above 2500 groups with 3.10 lakh women members with Rs. 85 crores corpus funds.

Infrastructure Development

Out of 1,098 revenue villages of the district 1,003 villages are inhabited and the rest of the villages are deserted. There are five towns in the district. The total length of surfaced roads in the district is 7,243 kms, and the total length of railway track (broad gauge) in the district is 153.84. Kms including 115 kms, of double line. Total population of the district is 35.22 lakhs out of which male 17.66 lakhs and female population is 17.75

lakhs. According to 2001 census, out of total population 4,57,679 (14.10%) are ST community. Total literates are 21.16 lakhs, male literacy rate is 68.61 and female literacy rate is 51.48. The Warangal city has considerably developed during the past three decades. The establishment of many new educational institution like Kakatiya University, NIT, KITS, Government polytechnic, Kakatiya Medical College, Government Ayuverdic College, ITI, Law college, Women's College, College of Education, Music and Dance School etc., besides the other private collages in all fields. The SDLCE has also added growth of education, culture in large section of population.

There are 3008 primary schools, 706 upper primary schools, 1153 zilla parishad schools are running in the district. Almost all educational institutions are poorly placed in infrastructural facilities. Such as pucca building, drinking water, electricity, sanitation, compound wall and play ground etc., the problem is acute in government. Institutions but is to say that the private schools are well equipped, these institutions are also suffering from may lacunas, among the total in the district 90 per cent schools are not having library and nearly 60 per cent schools are do not have electricity and sanitation facility. Nearly sixty per cent schools do not have drinking water, less than forty per cent schools have no proper boundary walls and more than forty per cent schools have no play ground. Even today we can find that classes are running under shade of the threes here and there in the district.

As far as quality aspects of school education is considered in general and particularly in this district much has to be done to improve the quality of education. The poor infrastructure facilities will have a direct bearence on the qualitative output from the schools. When the learning atmosphere is not conducive to the students it gives ample scope for drop-outs at various stages. It is high among the backward class community with 45-55 per cent.. There is 52.56 per cent drop-out found in the scheduled caste children. This has to be checked toughly to realise the dream universal education the government with the co-operation of NGOs, local philanthropists and elderly person establish working communities to mobilize funds to strengthen infrastructural facilities and to monitor the academic activity, proper accountability has to be fixed at various levels to the teachers and heads of the institutions to maintain and upgrade the standard of the institutions and to prepare the students in such a manner to face the emerging challenges of new socio-economic environment.

Education has become even more important today than before. An illiterate and low quality educated person cannot participate in the new knowledge based society driven by information technology. His/her exclusion will be total. Thus there is every need to bring about total literacy and to and process of learning at various levels and particularly in schools educations is should be made more qualitative such process should not confine only to the town a cities but should reach the rural neglected lot.

An analysis of Table 4.7 reveals that total child population of the Warangal district. Out of 6, 19,029 child populations in Warangal district, a majority of the child population 51.00 per cent are boys and 49.00 per cent girls. 16.98 per cent *i.e.* 1,05,1506 are Scheduled Caste (SC), 14.09 per cent *i.e.* 87,281 are Scheduled Tribe (ST) and remaining other communities. The ST and SC child population are almost equal. The observation showed that ST boys are higher compared to SC community. It is interesting to note that, out of total child population more than 51.75 per cent belong to 11-15 age group and less than 28.25 per cent belong to 6-10 age group.

The total enrolment students *i.e.* 6, 04,115, a majority of the children age group belong to 6-10 years and remaining were 11-15 age group. It is interesting to note that in Schedule Tribes total enrolment students *i.e.* 1,17,004 of which 60.12 per cent were belong to 6-10 age group in which 35,557 students are boys and 34,788 are girls remaining 59.88 per cent are belong to 11-15 age group in which 24,530 are boys and 22,129 are girls.

Table 4.7: Child Populations and Enrolment in Warangal District

Age Groups		All Communities			Schedule Caste			Schedule Tribes		
		6-10	11-15	Total	6-10	11-15	Total	6-10	11-15	Total
Child Population	Boys	152555	163151	315706	25960	27763	53723	21836	23353	45189
	Girls	146120	157174	303294	24774	26648	51422	20280	21814	42094
	Total	298701	320328	619029	50739	54411	105150	42116	45165	87281
Enrolment	Boys	162271	146148	308419	32192	27694	59886	35557	24530	60087
	Girls	152977	142719	295696	30813	28704	59517	34788	22129	56917
	Total	315248	288867	604115	63005	56398	119403	70345	46659	117004
Gross Enrl. Ration	Boys	106.37	90.89	98.63	124.01	101.53	112.77	162.84	107.57	135.20
	Girls	104.69	92.50	98.595	124.38	110.29	117.33	171.54	105.06	138.3
	Total	105.54	91.68	98.61	124.17	105.82	114.99	167.03	106.34	136.68

Source: Registrar General, India, Ministry of Home Affairs Government of India, New Delhi and DISE data 2010-11 (as on 30th Sept. 2010)

An analysis of Table 4.8 indicates that enrolment and out of school (drop-out) at primary level (I-V) in Warangal district. It is interesting to note that the highest 46.91 per cent drop-out recorded in schedule tribes, in which girls drop-out are very high *i.e.* 47.73. But it is observed that in Schedule Caste girls drop-out rate is low compared to boys, when we look in to the all communities the drop-out rate almost equal to boys and girls.

Table 4.8: Enrolments and Drop-out Rate at Primary Level (I-V) in Warangal District

		All Communities	Schedule Caste	Schedule Tribes
Enrolment in Class-I in 2007-08	Boys	42370	8373	11286
	Girls	40809	7981	11166
	Total	83179	16354	22452
Enrolment Classes-V in 2011-12	Boys	31357	6361	6083
	Girls	30279	6336	5837
	Total	61636	12697	11920
Drop-out Rate	Boys	25.99	24.03	46.10
	Girls	25.80	20.61	47.73
	Total	25.90	22.36	46.91

Source: Registrar General, India, Ministry of Home Affairs Government of India, New Delhi and DISE data 2010-11 (as on 30th Sept. 2010).

An analysis of Table 4.9 indicates that enrolment and out of school (drop-out) at upper primary level (I-VII) in Warangal district. It is interesting to note that the highest 59.47 per cent drop-out recorded in schedule tribes, in which girls drop-out are very high *i.e.* 60.28. But it is observed that in Schedule Caste and all communities girls drop-out rate is low compared to boys. When we observed the total drop-out rate is almost equal in SC and all communities.

Table 4.9: Enrolments and Drop-out Rate at Upper Primary Level (I-VII) in Warangal District

		All Communities	Schedule Caste	Schedule Tribes
Enrolment in Class-I in 2005-06	Boys	47651	9692	12867
	Girls	46341	9464	12630
	Total	93992	19156	25497
Enrolment in Classes-VII in 2011-12	Boys	30943	6037	5318
	Girls	30824	6273	5017
	Total	61767	12310	10335
Drop out Rate	Boys	35.06	37.71	58.67
	Girls	33.48	33.72	60.28
	Total	34.28	35.74	59.47

Source: Registrar General, India, Ministry of Home Affairs Government of India, New Delhi and DISE data 2010-11 (as on 30th Sept. 2010).

Table 4.10: Enrolments and Drop-out Rate at Secondary Level (I-X) in Warangal District

		All Communities	Schedule Caste	Schedule Tribes
Enrolment in Class-I in 2002-03	Boys	57477	11194	16078
	Girls	56039	10924	16381
	Total	113516	22118	32459
Enrolment in Classes-I-X in 2011-12	Boys	28182	5192	4342
	Girls	27029	5300	3725
	Total	55211	10492	8067
Drop-out Rate	Boys	50.97	53.62	72.99
	Girls	51.77	51.48	77.26
	Total	51.36	52.56	75.15

Source: Registrar General, India, Ministry of Home Affairs Government of India, New Delhi and DISE data 2010-11 (as on 30th Sept. 2010).

An analysis of Table 4.10 reveals that enrolment and out of school (drop-out) at secondary level (I-X) in Warangal district. It is interesting to note that the highest 75.15 per cent drop-out recorded in schedule tribes; in which girls drop-out are very high *i.e.* 77.26 and boys drop-out rate is 72.99 only. But it is observed that in Schedule Caste girls drop-out rate is low compared to boys. But in all communities indicates that girl's drop-out rate is higher than boys. When we observed the total drop-out rate is almost equal in SC and all communities.

Reasons for Drop-outs

The preceding analysis shows the existence of high drop-out rates at schools in Andhra Pradesh. In order to understand the causes for drop-outs and non-enrollment of children and also to identify the socio-economic barriers at the primary and secondary education a sample survey of 60 respondents *i.e.,* teachers, parents and students was undertaken to elicit their opinion on the causes for drop-outs in study area. Since local teacher's posses greater knowledge about the children, their parents and also about the local problems, we had selected then purposefully. The sample area also selected purposively representing different situations. This district represents urban and tribal conditions and presents a situation with low drop-out rates. As may as 78 respondents were randomly selected from this district. The sample is drawn from aided, unaided, government and private school teachers giving weightage to the experience and/or service of the teachers concerned, place of work etc., drop-out students and parents the opinions of these 60 respondents are tabulated and their views are presented below.

- Educational background of the parents.
- Poor economic conditions of the family.
- Excessive involvement of children in domestic work.
- Negligence of parents.
- Caste factor.

- Frequent shifting of the families, for seasonal work, from one place to other place for seeking livelihood, may also influence the drop-out rate.
- Due to ill health, like incidence of malaria fever, some of the student's drop-out from the schools.
- According to the teachers some of the students discontinued their studies due to lack of hostel facilities.
- Child marriages are also infecting the drop-out rate.

Conclusion and Suggestions

The above analysis envisages that education is one of the most important social indicators, which are directly linked with economic development. To increase the literacy levels in India in general and AP in particular, the state should concentrate on retention rather than enrolment especially schedule caste and schedule tribe communities to reduce social disparities. In addition to universal facilities, universal enrolment and universal retention, the availability of a universally high quality of teaching and learning should also be provided. Further, investment in education at all India level needs to be more than doubled from the present level 3.1 per cent of the GDP.

As a whole, the highest drop-out rate is recorded in the tribal community, As per the opinions elicited from the local teachers literacy levels of parents and poor economic conditions of the families are found to be the major reasons for drop-outs. Excessive involvement of children in domestic work, household chores, etc., and negligence of parents towards early marriages of girls children are the other causes for the higher drop-out rates. The policy implication of this study is obviously that the improvement in the economic status of poor families is the pre-condition far stopping drop-outs. In the short run, the government may consider the policy option of enrolling all the children of poor families in the residential schools compulsorily. These residential schools should be run on professional excellence.

Developing a very good infrastructure is a prerequisite of a good schooling system. This will make more attractive to students (Schools should be such were students like to spend more time instead of running away from it. Good infrastructure helps in making schools more interesting) which will help in increasing the enrolment in schools as well as improving the quality of education (Good infrastructure facilities like a well equipped computer laboratory with internet connection will help enormously in improving the quality of education).

REFERENCES

Banerji, R. (2000), "Poverty and Primary Schooling: Field Studies from Mumbai and Delhi, *Economic and Political Weekly, March.*

Census Reports, Director of Census Operations, Andhra Pradesh Reports, Various Year Economic Survey of India, 2011.

Hanushek, E. A. (2000), Schooling, Labour Force Quality and Growth of Nations. *The American Economic Review, 90*(5), 1184-1208.

Murali V. (2010), *"School Drop-out and Educational Facilities – A District Level Analysis in AP"* in *South Indian Journal of Social Science,* Vol. VIII No. 1 June, pp. 39-55.

Murali V., *et al*, (2005), *"Educational Opportunities in a Village Economy – A Micro Level Study"*, Published in AP Economic Association XXIII Annual Conference Volume, 2005.

Outcome Budget 2009-10, Department of Tribal Welfare, Andhra Pradesh. Also available online at http://www.aptribes.gov.in/

Performance Appraisal System of Tribal Welfare, Andhra Pradesh, January, 2003.

Performance Appraisal System, Tribal Welfare Department, Andhra Pradesh: Guidelines for Preparation of Action Plans, January, 2002.

Performance Appraisal System, Tribal Welfare Department, Andhra Pradesh: Guidelines for Preparation of Department Action Plans at Unit Level, January, 2002.

Rao, D. P, (2005), *"Drop-outs in Primary Education in East Godavari District of Andhra Pradesh – Mandal Level Analysis"*, Published in AP Economic Association XXIII Annual Conference Volume, 2005.

School Education Department Reports 2011-12.

Sury, M. M. (2004), Indian Economy in the 21st Century, New Century Publications, New Delhi.

Tilak, Jandhya B.G (2004), "Education in the UPA Government Common Minimum Programme, *Economic and Political Weekly*, 23rd Oct, 2004.

5

Livelihood Issues of De-notified, Nomadic and Semi-Nomadic Tribes
Displacement, Relocation and Rehabilitation

1. Uttam Madane

ABSTRACT

India being a democratic country embedded with the values of fraternity, equality, and liberty in its society and the constitution assures the dignity, equity and freedom of people although there are social categories prevalent at large in the society generally known as ST, SC, OBC, and religious minority groups. However, besides this categorisation, still some section of people, who did not find place in anyone of the previously mentioned categorisation rather separately identified as Nomadic and De-notified Tribes constitute approximately 60 million population of India. They are identified and categorised in different social categories in different states of India. The NT-DNTs are one of the marginalized sections of the society, who are excluded from the mainstream of development since pre-independence to till date.

1. M.Phil Scholar, School of Social Work, Tata Institute of Social Sciences, Deonar, Mumbai - 400 088.

This paper attempts to provide the insights about their struggle for livelihood and unawareness about the contemporary development programmes. It has been noticed that they are deprived of being benefited from the various welfare schemes, as they do not have citizenship identity proof. At present, their livelihood depends on their traditional occupation like animal playing on the street, snake charmer, an acrobat, musicians, begging in the name of God etc. However in developing country like India, the process of liberalization, privatization, globalisation policies and laws has made development scenario more complex for NT-DNTs in terms of their social-economic status, cultural life and livelihood resources and in turn this led to poverty, unemployment and forceful deprivation of access to natural resources. People have lost their livelihood resources and they cannot get in to new emerging jobs due to lack of particular skills required for currently booming jobs in the market. This community has been unattended in government's appropriate and sufficient welfare policies and development programmes since independence. The findings indicates that lacuna of accessibility to these development programme continues these communities to be excluded and discriminated in the society as well as government concern.

Introduction

India is not just an ordinarily democratic country but it's a democratic country based on social and humanistic perspectives. Indian constitution has given safeguard to all its citizens and emphasised its marginalized section of the society for their welfare, which considered Scheduled Castes, Scheduled Tribes, Other Backward Classes, Special Economic Backward Classes, Women, People with Disabilities and Minorities to create an equal platform for all. The Constitution made a provision to include the rest of the unscheduled population for further welfare programmes for their upliftment which was not taken further seriously by the government in its follow up which brought into result that, the communities like De-notified and Nomadic Tribe could not involved for direct beneficial programmes for their welfare due to the negligence of further government procedure as per the constitution and also found ignorance from communities those are remained out.

Nomadic and De-notified Tribes cover approximately of 60 million populations in India (Rathod, 2000). India is going towards stage of developed countries but still NT-DNTs are one of the marginalized social categories, which excluded from mainstream of development since pre-independence. NT-DNTs live with stigma of criminality labeled by British Government under the Criminal Tribe Act of 1871 as well as way of nomadic life in search of livelihood with struggling police as well as societies' violence.

These communities are struggling for their livelihood sources in society. Their livelihood has depended on their traditional occupation, *e.g.*, animal playing on the street, snake-charmer, an acrobat, musicians, begging on the name of God etc. However, in developing country like India, even the process of globalisation has made development scenario much more complex in terms of NT-DNT's social-economic, cultural life and livelihood resources and its strongly leading to poverty, unemployment, and lack of access to resources. People are losing their traditional livelihood resources and beside due to the stigma and lack of required skills; they are not getting new job also. These communities unattended from government welfare policies and programmes since independence. Thus, these communities are remained excluded and discriminated in social and economical safeguard point of view from both society and government and they are struggling for livelihoods.

Numerous tribes across the world continue to wander from place to place for satisfying their biogenic needs of food, clothing and shelter, which they attempt to fulfill through hunting, agriculture, herding, etc. Therefore, they are commonly known as 'Nomadic tribes' (Ghatage, 2006). De-notified Tribes known as *'vimukta jati' as well as "Ex-criminal Tribes"*. De-notified Tribes are those communities, which had originally listed under the Criminal Tribes Act of 1871 by British government. In modern settled way of life has seen as common, universal, and life of nomadic in simple way a life of migrating from one place to another in search of livelihood has seen the trait of backwardness. The concept of modern settled way of life is seen to be superior in comparison with nomadic way of life in which their livelihood is based their own sources of production.

There are 313 Nomadic Tribes and 198 De-notified Tribes in India, out of these 28 Nomadic Tribes and 14 De-notified tribes find in Maharashtra, which constitute about five million of population in Maharashtra and about 60 million all over India (Rathod, M. 2000). Due to the wandering traditions over hundreds of years without any ostensible means of livelihood under the influence of the caste system, they are continuously forced to live under sub human conditions.[1] There are so many, who are powerless and oppressed; where NT-DNTs are one of them.

Citizenship Rights and Livelihood

De-notified, Nomadic and Semi Nomadic Tribes are struggling for their citizenship rights in Indian democratic country. According to Marshall, T. H (1977), the citizenship right has constructed in three components, that is, civil, political, and social right (Marshall, 1977). If we overlook the situation of De-notified, Nomadic and Semi Nomadic tribes since ancient period, It shows in case of civil rights that this people are far away from individual freedom, right to liberty of the person, right to justice (Right to justice means right to be treated in terms of equality), because, they cannot live on one place for long time due to lack of livelihood resources which is depend on their traditional occupation as well as society do not accept them in their residencies for long time because of stigma of criminality has attached to them. Still they are wondering with the stigma of criminality under the mainstream societies' influence. These things are affecting on their livelihoods and they are getting loss from their traditional livelihood. The political participation of NT-DNTs is also discouraging. They are deprived basic political rights. Political right means right to participate in the exercise of political power as a member of a body vested with political authority such as the parliament or their counterparts at the regional and local level. It also means right to participate in the process whereby members exercising the political authority are elected. However, De-notified, Nomadic and Semi Nomadic tribes are in nomadic nature and they do not have residence of particular place and citizenship documents such as Voter ID, Ration Card etc., because of which they cannot be recognise as a citizenship of country then how do they can fulfill their political right? Always they have remained excluded from government facilities and welfare services because of lack of citizenship documents which it required for accessing such government welfare services, *e.g.*, under PDS (Public Distribution System), Government of India distributes subsidised food and non-food items to India's poor, major commodities distributed include staple food grains, such as wheat, rice, sugar, and kerosene through a network of public distribution shops established in several state across the country. But without ration card they cannot take advantage of this government services and there are chunk of population of De-notified, Nomadic and semi Nomadic tribes have in country without citizenship documents such as ration card, Voter ID, Caste Certificate. This is just one example. Government provide many services to poor but it is not reaching to actual poor of this country and in case of NT-DNTs because do not having citizenship documents. Social right means right to modicum of economic welfare and security to the right to the full in the social heritage, which means right to live a life of a civilized being according to the standard prevailing in the society (Marshall 1977:78), but these communities' existence has refused by society. They cannot stay near (out of village) the village more than three days. When these people come near the village in search of their livelihood that time villagers make public announcement in village that theft has come near village be alert[2] (Rathod, 2012:37). Then how do they enjoy the social right? If people see them by biased attitude, how do they get their livelihood from that village? Due to this types of reason De-notified, Nomadic and Semi Nomadic Tribes are getting trouble to get livelihoods by begging, entertaining people through physical dexterity, providing services to people like wood basket, Ayurvedik Medicine, stone things etc., which is depend on the other people's response to them.

Education and Livelihood

Due to the wandering tradition, De-notified, Nomadic and Semi Nomadic Tribes cannot take education from the regular school systems in a settled society. Education is a mirage to the De-notified Nomadic and Semi Nomadic communities. It is no wonder that these communities are largely illiterate and those who are educated are educated mostly up to 10th class[3] (National Commission for De-notified, Nomadic and Semi Nomadic tribes Report, 2008). Kratli writes that from the point of view of official education nomads are a complete failure: in terms of enrolment, attendance, classroom performance, gender equations, and dropout rates, they continue to be at the bottom of the ladder (Krätli, 2001. Cited from Consortium for Research on Education Access, Transitions, and Equity – South Asian Nomads – Literature Review, funded by DFID). However, although some of them are poor, they are far from being a drifting, unskilled underclass as they presumably should be without formal education. Education is a basic agent of change in the process of socio-economic development of disadvantage group. De-notified, Nomadic and Semi nomadic tribes are no exception. The government of India recently made education a fundamental right for every child between 6 and 14 on April 2010 through The Right of Children to Free and Compulsory Education. Education is presented both as a fundamental right (with its inclusion in the Universal Declaration of Human Rights in 1948) and as a way towards economic and social empowerment. Nomadic groups passed on their socio cultural and economic knowledge to their children to pursue their traditional occupation without recourse to non-indigenous education. Over the last few decades, nomadic and De-notified groups have had to deal with rapid changes to their way of life, often a consequence of an increasingly globalising world in which development measures remains highly unsympathetic to De-notified, nomads and Semi nomadic tribe. They are going to lose their traditional occupation and they do not have good education background, which is not helping them to get in new job for their livelihood. Lack of education among the communities' leads to unemployment, superstation, and its lead to poverty among them.

Government's Effort and Livelihood

Since, ancient period these people's existence has refused by society and the government System at the same time these tribes have never been registered anywhere. These communities are far away from fulfilling their social, economical, educational, and political rights. Several commissions and committees has appointed for studying on De-notified, Nomadic and Semi Nomadic Tribes at state as well as national level, *e.g. Criminal Tribe Inquiry Committee - 1947, Ayyangar Committee - 1949, Kalelkar commission - 1953, Lokur Committee - 1965, Mandal Commission - 1980, Justice Venkatachalih Commission even Start committee, Segmintan Committee, All India Jail Commission, Munshi Commission, Dr. Antrolikar commission, Thade Commission.*

They gave their recommendation, but nothing is resulted at implementation level. *Start committee, Segmintan Committee, All India Jail Commission, Munshi Commission, Dr. Antrolikar commission, Thade Commission* has given recommendations that Nomadic and De-notified Tribes should include in Schedule Tribe. After this, all commissions and committees, Maharashtra state government appointed Justice R. N. Bapat Commssion for study of NT-DNTs of Maharashtra State. This commission made study tour in Maharashtra for doing survey of these communities and submitted the recommendation to Maharashtra Government. Commission has done in detail study of criminal tribes since 1793 as well as study of Criminal Tribe Act 1871 and review of 1860 Indian Pinal Code or 1861 Criminal Procedure Code. How has one tribe included under different schedule? Commission had brought in to notice that is how bureaucracy has in disarray as well as irresponsible for it. *Lamani, Berad (Bedar), Bhamata/Pardeshi/Bantibori, Bhilla, Kaikadi/Korah, Manggarudi, Pardhi, Sannsi, Tadvi, Charanbanjara in Haidrabad and Banjara in Middle India* has included in Schedule Caste. Currently *Bhilla* has included under Schedule Caste in Maharashtra. *Banjara and Laman* are included under De-notified tribes. Kaikadi has included in Schedule Caste in Vidarbha region of Maharashtra but in remaining parts of Maharashtra, it has come under the De-notified Tribes. Commission has indicated that distributions of tribes in schedule are contradictory and peculiar. *Pardhi* Tribe listed under Schedule Tribes in North Maharashtra as well as Vidarbha region of Maharashtra but it has included in De-notified Tribe in remaining parts of Maharashtra.

Sixty-five years down the line since India is independent, there is a stark scarcity of development, especially among the vulnerable De-notified, Nomadic and Semi Nomadic communities. As far as present development is concerned India's economic growth rate has reached to 9.2 per cent GDP, but at the same time, there seems a less inclusion of the De-notified, Nomadic and Semi Nomadic communities in the process of development. In the era of globalisation and due to other factors, De-notified, Nomadic and Semi Nomadic communities continue to be neglected from development process and their rights are unfulfilled.

State is responsible for the economical and educational development of communities being oppressed[4] (Article number 46 in Indian constitution). According to these provisions, the state is also responsible for giving them protection from exploitation. As per the constitutional provision, Maharashtra government has established the directorate of The NT-DNT and Social Justice and Special Cooperative Division. In 1984, under the control of Directorate of NT/DNT's and Social Justice and Special Co-operative Division, the Government of Maharashtra has established the Vasantrao Naik Vimukta Jati and Nomadic Tribes Development Corporation for the upliftment and overall development of NT/DNTs. The Aim of this Corporation is an economic upliftment of the persons belonging to Vimukta Jatis and Nomadic Tribes by giving loan to this people on concessional rate.[5] Under the Vasantrao Naik Vimukta Jatis and Nomadic Tribes Development Corporation have some schemes funded by Government of Maharashtra, such as: *Beej Bhandwal karj yojana, Thet karj Yojana* and *Anudan Yojana, Mudat Karj Yojana, Marjin Mani Karja Yojana, swayamsaksham karj Yojana, swarnima karj Yojana, micro credit karj yojana, Mahila Samrudhi Karj Yojana, and prashikshan karj yojana.* Corporation is making available a loan through the bank for the economical development and self-business. NT-DNT communities are always wondering from one place to another place, so access to these schemes is very limited.[6] People do not have caste certificate, ration card, voter ID; therefore, they cannot complete requirements of documents for access the scheme of VNVJNTDC. Compare to approximately population of NT-DNTs and allocated budget to VNVJNTDC is very less. Another thing is that whatever money is proving through corporation to each scheme is very less in today's dearth. Purpose of each scheme has not fulfilled through allocated budget of each scheme. That is why people are not able to sustain their enterprises/purpose by accessing the schemes of Development Corporation. Many schemes have announced through Development Corporation but due to the limited budget only *Bij Bhandawal Karja Yojana* is running in current year 2012-13.[7] The benefits are accessed from Vasantrao Naik Vimukta Jati And Nomadic Tribe Development Corporation are very limited. The various reasons are affecting on the access of developmental schemes, such as not have hold of ration card, voter identity card, caste certificate, unawareness regarding scheme access process.[8] Development Corporation implement training scheme under this Scheme Training Fee and Stipend provided for 6 month Training for Audio/Video Repairing, Plumbing, Welding, Construction, Motor Driving, Beauty Parlor, Carpenter and Mobile Repairing etc., its good opportunities to De-notified, Nomadic and Semi-Nomadic tribes people for getting their livelihood but lack of citizenship documents they cannot access schemes. Another important thing is that those people have citizenship documents they applied for such schemes and they have gotten sanction since two three years but still they did not received money from development corporation and related Banks[9] (Dr. Bavane, L. 1992:55). Some people got loan from Development Corporation, those who was able to keep follow up and visited to Mumbai office continuously. But compared to received amount from corporation under scheme and spending money to accessing process of scheme or traveling to Mumbai office for continuous follow up of application and during this mental harassed are not countable in satisfaction (Bavane, L. 1992:55). If situation is like this then how does people get benefit of Development Corporation's scheme and sustain their livelihood through such schemes.

At the same time due to the less education and not effective skills, they are also not able to get employment opportunities in the jobs. Therefore, in this situation the role of the VNVJNTDC (Vasantrao Naik Vimukta Jatis and Nomadic Tribes Development Corporation ltd.) is very significant for providing the loans, training for sustaining their own business and getting employment opportunities. However, it is not happening in practical situation due to not having regularly budge allocation to Vasantrao Naik Vimukta Jatis and Nomadic Tribes Development Corporation ltd.

Liberalization, Privatization and Globalisation Policies/Laws and Livelihood

Due to the LPG policies and new economic development policies and laws, the traditional occupations of these communities are not able to sustain, therefore they are finding it quite difficult to get in to other occupations. Basically V. Raghaviah (1968) has divided these communities by their occupation in some categories in his Nomads book namely: the food gathering nomads, pastoral nomads, trader nomads, criminal nomads and beggar nomads and Milind Bokil has divided these communities in four categories by their occupation namely: *(i)* hunter gatherers, *(ii)* good and services nomads, *(iii)* entertainers nomads and *(iv)* religious nomads. Some NT-DNTs communities traditional occupation are bull deckers, Snake charmers, Monkey trainers, Bear Trainers and their livelihood is totally depend on the this traditional occupation but Government's new policies and laws are affecting on the livelihood of de-notified, Nomadic and Semi-Nomadic tribe. Wildlife protection Act of 1972 has come and hunter-gatherers communities loosed their livelihood. These NT-DNTs communities used to hunting of fowl, rabbits, deer, monkeys etc., and gathering bark, roots, tubers, corns, leaves, flowers, seeds, frits, sap, honey, toddy and other forest products for their livelihood. Hunting of wild animals has been prohibited under Sec. 9 of the Wildlife (P) Act, 1972. No person is allowed to hunt any wild animal specified in Schedule I, II, III and IV except as provided under sections 11 and 12 of the Act. The Act also prohibits under section 17A, the collection or the trade in specified plants (whether alive or dead or part or derivative) *i.e.,* those listed in Schedule VI of the Act, from any forest land and any area specified by notification by the Central Government.[10] The Prevention of Cruelty to Animals Act, 1960 has come and animal performers' communities loosed their traditional occupation. Article 51A of the Constitution provides for fundamental duties of every citizen. When sub-clause (g) of article 51A provides "to protect and improve the natural environment including forest, lakes, rivers and wild life and to have compassion for living creatures and sub-clause (h) provides "to develop the scientific temper, humanism and the spirit of inquiry and reforms" as fundamental duties.

Against this backdrop the Prevention of Cruelty to Animals Act, 1960 was enacted not only to prevent the animals from all types of cruelty, but also to protect their existence as Constitutional obligation. On the other hand, to maintain ecological balance on the earth, the existence of animals is necessary. However, section 28 of the Act provides exemption for inflicting cruelty and killing to animals in the name of religion or for performing religious rites. It is unfortunate because nowhere in the religious textbooks it is mentioned that killing animals is necessary for religious ceremonies. Killing of a living being for religious purpose is not only against the spirit of the Constitution and law, but also against the tenets of any religion.[11] Thus, these communities excluded from their livelihood and now they do not have any alternative for livelihood and it is leading to poverty.

Some of the Nomadic and de-notified communities used to begging for their survival but they have been banned from doing such things under The Bombay Prevention of Begging Act (BPBA), 1959. Which was made for Bombay (now Mumbai) was extended to Delhi in March 1961. For carrying out the purposes of the Act, Delhi Prevention of Begging Rules 1960 and Delhi Prevention of Begging (Amendment) Rules in 1962 were also been framed. The Department of Social Welfare (DSW), Government of National Capital Territory of Delhi (GNCTD) in its background note stated; "the said Act makes begging at public places a crime and a punishable offence.[12] Due to this Act, these communities loosed their survival sources as well as they do not have any special skills to get in any other new job for their livelihood. These situations are leading to get into criminal activities and again they are becoming the victim of police system. However, they do not have any alternatives for their livelihoods.

Some of the Nomadic and de-notified communities such as *Dombari, Kolhati, Bahurupi, Nandiwala, Garudi, Makadwala, Madari etc.,* used to entertaining people through strolling actors, wrestler, jugglers, danseuses, picture showmen, acrobats. They were entertaining people on the street by doing such activities, but in the process of liberalization, privatization and globalisation some other entertainment facilities came such as spread of cinema, TV and other modern entertainment media. Therefore, people got easy and qualitative entertainment programmes on electronic media. That is why day by day people's interest and response to entertaining activities of these communities become less. Due to this, reason people loosed their traditional occupation and got deprive from livelihood resources.

Some of the nomadic and de-notified communities used to begging on the name of God such as *Gosavi, Wasudeo, Davari, Bharadi, Masanjogi etc.* Such communities used to worship of God and people consider them as a God's messenger but they beg for their survival. However, in the process of modernization, rationality is spreading; superstition is losing as well as it form is changing, that is why these communities are not entertaining by people. Thus, they are losing their occupation and going in livelihood crises and strongly it is leading to poverty. At the same time they do not have any skills to get in new job as well as they do not have aware about importance of education. These situations are affecting on their next generation. They do not send their children in school and practically it is not possible because of their nomadic nature life. So next generation are in complex situation about their future life. They do not get in their traditional occupation because of its going to destroy and getting trouble to get in new skill base job because they do not have education and require training for that particular job. Thus, these communities are struggling for their livelihood.

Some of the nomadic and de-notified communities such as *Vaidu, Banjara, Shikkalgar, Kanjarbhat, Beldar, Ghisadi, Patharwat, Chapparband, Kaikadi, Mati Wadar, Otari, Sangar etc.*, used to provide good and services to the people such as handmade wool cloths, wood basket, *ayurvedik* medicine, local liquor, stone gadget, wool blanket etc., due to mechanization and industrialisation, these communities loss their traditional occupation. Industrial production captured whole urban and rural market with better quality production compare to handmade production, however, demand of these people's production has decreased automatically and its lead to livelihood crises among this group of people.

Some De-notified communities' have strong historical background of warriors, for instant *Ramoshi/Berad/Bedar* communities. During Shivaji Maharaj Kingdom, this people were in administration as well as in army of Chhatrapati Shivaji Maharaj. They were working as a detective for Shivaji Maharaj. In Maratha period, the Ramoshi/Berad/Bedar came to addressed as 'Naik' which means 'Leader'. In addition, they were engaged in the protection of forts and rendered the very valuable service of espionage. During British Period, they fought against British for freedom under the leadership of Umaji Naik who was belonged to same community. This community has brave historical background however, they got gratuity land, but some smart, selfish people have taken benefit of this community's illiteracy and creaulity. They took out land of this people from them. Now maximum people of this communities are landless however they loss their livelihood resources. *Ramoshi, Berad, and Bedar* communities' have same socio-cultural characteristics but region wise they known by different name. They known by *Ramoshi* name in Maharashtra and by *Berad or Bedar* name in Karnataka.

Political Representation and Livelihood

Due to lack of proper political representation at expected level, these communities are excluded in the policy level decisions, discourses, and budget provision in state. Article 46 of the Constitution laid down the Directive Principle that the State shall promote with special care the educational and economic interests of the weaker sections of the people and, in particular, of scheduled castes and scheduled tribes, and shall protect them from social injustice and all forms of exploitation. As per this provision; in the first five-year plan, out of total provision of Rs. 39 crores for the welfare of backward classes, there was just made provision of Rs. 3.5 crores a beginning was made for the resettlement of ex-criminal tribes (De-notified, Nomadic and Semi Nomadic Tribes) and for training them in the ways of settled community life. The second five-year plan allocates a total amount of about Rs. 91 crores for the welfare of backward classes and there was made provision of Rs. 4 crores for programmes which are – specially designed to assist De-notified, Nomadic and Semi Nomadic tribes. The programme for ex-criminal tribes (De-notified, Nomadic and Semi Nomadic Tribes), for which a provision of Rs. 2.94 crores has been made in the second plan, includes schemes of colonization and rehabilitation of people, most of whom – are still leading a nomadic life. Since the de-notification of tribes, formerly described as 'criminal', some schemes for their rehabilitation and development have been taken up in the States but nothing in result and in implementation. There had made budget allocates amount of about Rs. 114 crores in the Third five-year plan for the welfare of backward classes, but only provides Rs. 4 crores to De-notified, Nomadic and semi nomadic Tribes as against the anticipated outlay during the First and the Second Plans of about Rs. 1 crore and Rs. 2.9 crores respectively. There had been provision of Rs. 4.5 crores in fourth five year plan with combined-cum-welfare approach supported by schemes of general education, social education, economic uplift and housing for the De-notified, Nomadic and Semi Nomadic Tribes. There were no budgetary allocation for De-notified, Nomadic and Semi Nomadic Tribes in fifth five-year plan. Government has mentioned to De-notified, Nomadic and Semi Nomadic Tribes, as a part of budget in sixth five-year plan but it was not cleared that how much budget was for De-notified, Nomadic and Semi Nomadic Tribes. After these plans, there was nothing special in seventh five-year plan to tenth five-year plan for De-notified, Nomadic and Semi Nomadic Tribes. In midterm appraisal of 11th five-year plan, the planning commission of India allocates the budget for education and economic development of the NT-DNT under the schedule caste special component plan (Midterm Appraisal of 11th Five-year Plan – Social Sector Report). However, if we look the ratio of amount provided to welfare of backward classes and out of that to De-notified, Nomadic and Semi Nomadic Tribes is very contrast. Whatever amount government had provide in the first five-year plan to eleventh five-year plan for welfare of backwards classes was increasing but compare to total amount of welfare of backward classes and amount of De-notified, Nomadic and Semi Nomadic has not increased according to total amount of backward classes. Thus, these communities has excluded at planning level in the democratic country. Thus, since independence to till date government has not taken the any effectively initiative for their livelihood and settlement. There are no any provision of livelihood for De-notified, Nomadic and Semi-Nomadic Tribes in five-year plan of India. First time government of Maharashtra has budgetary allocation for settlement of Denotified and nomadic Tribes in the state. The new scheme going to launch for their settlement namely "Yeshwantrao chavan Mukti (free) settlement scheme for DNT's" in 12th five-year plan (Kambale M: 2011).

NT-DNT communities were missing from the demographic analysis because of missing from census enumeration. There is not correct population of NT-DNT's, few studies and author told estimated population of DNT's. The criminal Tribes Act enquiry committee (1949-50) recorded 34,87,597 person as belonging to 127 communities. With the growth of the population during the last some decades, the population of these communities has gone up, and it is estimated at about five million.[13] National commission for De-notified, Nomadic and semi Nomadic tribes recorded estimate population at about 10,74,50,018.[14] On the bases of particular group's population (one criteria), Planning commission make the budget provision for welfare of such category and still government don't have the exactly population of De-notified, Nomadic and Semi Nomadic Tribes in India and it is very serious concern for exclusion of this communities at planning and Programme level.

Conclusion: The Alternatives

As far, as all over situation is concerned, their socio-economic, educational, and political development not seems at the expected level. These communities are away from basic rights of citizenship. There are not having enough constitutional safe guards and effective governments' policies for mainstreaming this community.[15] These people are suffering because of liberalizations, privatization and globalisation policies and laws, which is affecting on their socio-cultural, life and livelihood. There is no any alternative to them for overcoming on their livelihood problems. This communities entangled in very worst misery because of Government's negligence at policy and planning level as well as community's attitude towards them as criminalized people. They are living invisible in democratic country.

Development should be holistic concept that encompasses the progressive improvement in the quality of human life in terms of food, clothing and shelter and the conditions for the healthy living with increasing longevity of life and happiness. De-notified, Nomadic and Semi-Nomadic Tribes are included in Schedule Tribes, Schedule Caste, and other Backward Class in different-different state of India. These people cannot take the benefit of development schemes of that particular state. All De-notified, Nomadic and Semi-Nomadic Tribes are fulfilling the criteria, which is listed for Schedule Tribes such as Primitive Traits, Distinct Cultural Identity, Geographical Isolation, Social Backwardness, Common Gods, Worship, common customs, dialect etc., excepting residence of particular place. Therefore, these people should include in Schedule Tribes list in overall India and should make the provision of separate welfare schemes for their development.

Chunk of population of De-notified, Nomadic and Semi Nomadic Tribes are without Citizenship Documents such as Caste Certificate, Voter ID and Ration Card etc., which is depriving them to take the Benefit of some welfare schemes, and Public Distribution System's services, which is very necessary to overcoming their starvation. Still government does not have the survey data of these people. Therefore, government should start to take initiative for issuing the citizenship documents as well as collecting the survey data of these people. There should be provision of special component plan in five-year plan for mainstreaming development of De-notified, Nomadic and Semi Nomadic tribes like schedule Tribes and Schedule Caste.

These people are going to lose their traditional occupation because of Policies and laws of liberalization, privatization and globalisation. Therefore, Government should provide skill base education, health care facilities, as well as sustainable food supply to improve their quality of life. These needs can be fulfilled by pursuing a sustainable development model that ensures growth with equity and provide employment for all.

These people do not have permanent residence. They are in Nomadic nature. Therefore, government should provide land and houses to them with all basic facilities. There are the need of opening more school for their children and should provide scholarship to them. Government should provide loan and training to people through Vasantrao Naik Vimukta Jati and Nomadic Tribes Development Corporation for starting and sustaining small skill industries.

FOOTNOTES

1. Rathod, M. 2000, Denotified and Nomadic Tribes in Maharashtra http://sickle.Bwh.harvard.edu /india_ ztribes. html.
2. NT-DNT people had compulsion for giving attendance to village's police patil two time in a day. The time of attendance was inconvenience. They used to give attendance at 11pm and 3am in the night. Therefore, they used to awake whole night. There were illiterate and could not understand the time at night timing that is why whole night they stay near the police patil's house.
3. NT-DNT communities have poor access to education due to the problem of livelihood security and sustenance. Children are initiated into income earning activities at very tender age.
4. The State shall promote with special care the educational and economic interests of the weaker sections of the people, and, in particular, of the Scheduled Castes and the Scheduled Tribes, and shall protect them from social injustice and all forms of exploitation.
5. Vasantrao Naik Vimukta Jati and Nomadic Tribes Development Corporation (www.vnvjntdc.org).
6. Discussion with officers of Vasantarao Naik Vimukta Jati and Nomadic Tribes Development Corporation, Pune Division office, Pune.
7. Discussion with officers of Vasantarao Naik Vimukta Jati and Nomadic Tribes Development Corporation, Pune Division office, Pune.

8. ECONET presentation to planning commission, 2011 (ECONET is NGO working for NT-DNT issues).
9. Thus, Development Corporation have new strategy for exploitation of people by delaying to give justice them. In 1989, Development Corporation had started 50 per cent subsidy scheme for these people's development, but what happen in between don't know and these scheme has stopped.
10. Wildlife Protection Act of 1972.
11. The prevention of Cruelty to Animals (Amendment) Bill, 2011. By Shri Mohan Jena, M. P. Bill No. 67 of 2011.
12. The Bombay Prevention of Begging Act, 1959.
13. Bharal, G.P. (1968). De-notified communities and their Problems of Rehabilitation, *Indian Journal of Social Work*, Volume XXVIII, No. 4, Mumbai.
14. National Commission for De-notified, Nomadic and Semi Nomadic Tribes, 2008.
15. ECONET presentation to planning commission, 2011. Econet as an organization (NGO) is working on the issues of De-notified, Nomadic and Semi Nomadic Tribes.

REFERENCES

Bharal, G.P. 1968, *De-notified Communities and their Problems of Rehabilitation*. The Indian Journal of Social Work, Vol, 28, TISS, Mumbai.

Bokil, M. 2002. *De-Notified and Nomadic Tribes: A Perspective*. http://www.jst or. org /stable/4411599

Dilip D'Souza. 2001. *Branded by Law; Looking at Indian's De-notified Tribes*. New Delhi.

Dilip D'Souza.'nd'. *Declared Criminal at Birth, India's "De-notified Tribes"*. *http://www.manushi.in/docs/414.%20Declared%20Criminal%20at%20Birth.pdf*

Dr. Bavane, L. 2005, *Bhatakyancha Bhagna Sansar Ani Sanskruti*, Vardha Sudhir Publication.

Dr. Jamanadas, K. 2003, Criminal Tribes of India, *http://www.ambedkar.org/jamanadas/ CriminalTribes.htm*

Enthoven, R. E. 1975, *Tribes and Caste of Bombay*, Vol. III, Cosmo Publication, Delhi.

Enthoven, R.E., 1975, *Tribes and Caste of Bombay*, Vol. I, Cosmo Publication, Delhi.

Ghatage, B.S. 2006, *Nomadic Tribes, and Social Work in India*, Shruti Publication, Jaipur.

Haan, A.de. and Kabeer, N. 2008. *Social Exclusion; two Essays*, Critical Quest, New Delhi.

Information for the *Consideration of the Committee on the Elimination of Racial Discrimination* in Reviewing *India's 15th to 19th Periodic Reports*, February - 2007, *http://www2.ohchr.org/english/bodies/cerd/docs/ngos/resist.pdf*

Kambale, M. 2011, *Upekshit Samajasathi Bhariv Tartud; Navya Yojanancha Matra Abhav*, Mumbai: Sakal News Paper.

Kharat, S. 2003, *Bhatakya Vimukta Jamati va Tyanche Prashna*, Pune: Sugava Publication.

Lalitha, V and Gandhi, M. 2001. *The Status of Denotified Communities after Indian Independence, A Case Study of Andhra Pradesh*. Journal of Rural Development, Vol. 20(1), NIRD, Hyderabad.

Mane, L.1997, *Vimuktayan*: Maharashtratil *Vimukta Jamati-Ek Chikitsak Abhyas*, Mumbai: Yeshawantrao Chavan Pratisthan.

Moretti, M. (nd), Internatinal laws and Nomadic People, http:/www.iehei.org/biblioth eque/NOMADIC%20PEOPLE.pdf

Pal Sing, B. 2010, *Defining the Tribes: The De-notified Tribes of Punjab*. The Eastern Anthropologist.

Paul Appasamy, S. Guhan, R. Mujumdar, H. M and Vaidyanathan, A. 1996. *Social Exclusion from Welfare Rights Perspective in India*, International Institute of Labour Studies.

Radhakrishna, M. 2001. *Dishonoured by History 'Criminal Tribes' and British Colonial Policy*. Orient Lonaman Limited, New Delihi.

Ragvaviah, V. 1968. *Nomads*. Bharateeya Adim Jati Seva Sangha, New Delhi.

Rathod, M. 2012. *Gunhegar Jamati Kayda Aani Parinam*. Nirman and Ashmak Org, Pune.

Rathod, M., 2000, *Denotified and Nomadic Tribes in Maharashtra http://sickle.bwh.harvard.edu/india_tribes.html*

Simhadri, Y. C. 1973, *Ex-criminal Tribes and Criminological Theories*. The Indian Journal of Social Work, Vol. 34, TISS, Mumbai.

Simhadri, Y.C. 1977, *Caste and Denotified Tribes*. The Indian Journal of Social Work, Vol. 37, TISS, Mumbai.

Simhadri, Y. C. 1978, *Differential Association and Denotified Tribes*. The Indian Journal of Social Work, Vol. 39, TISS, Mumbai.

Simhadri, Y. C. 1991, *De-notified Tribes (A Sociological Analysis)*. Classical Publishing Company, New Delhi.

Singh K. S. 1998, *People of India – Indian National Series Volume VI – Indian Communities N – Z*. Delhi, Oxford University Press.

Vasantrao Naik Vimukta Jati and Nomadic Tribe Development Corporation Ltd. http://www.vnvjntdc.com/

6

Barriers of Tribal Students in Pursuing Primary Education

1. N. Kalpana Kumari

Tribes are the most vulnerable section of the socio-economic fabric. They still live a primitive life when compared with the rest of the civilized world. The tribal people are suffers from, poverty, illiteracy. Innocence, and exploitation and their development is retarded due these factors and lack of awareness. The S.T population accounts for 6.31 per cent in the state out of total population of Andhra Pradesh. The overall development of Tribal should be include the change in educational, social, economic, political aspects while keeping and consolidating their special identify of culture, habitation, tradition and in terms of their primitive rights and privilege. Particularly education of tribes is considered significant not only constitutional obligations but also important input for their total development. But the efforts of government is not fruitful because of wastage and stagnation in the area, There

1. ICPR - Junior Research Fellow, Department of Education, Andhra University. E-mail: kalpanakumari8276@gmail.com

is need to study the facilitating factors for their drop-out, non-retention and non-enrollment.

John Jacob (1983) observed that lack of education stumbling block in the tribes. Though some of the tribal settlements have elementary school within short distance and free education many tribal parents refrain children to schools, because loss of work force, expenditure and awareness on need of education. Laxminarayana (1984) observed that the reasons for not attending schooling are due to work at home, health problems, lack of proper clothing, reading and writing material.

Khuran, O. K (1978) in his article entitled 'Approach to education to Tribes' pointed out that in spite of all the efforts to reduce the illiteracy among the scheduled tribes the gap exists because of their poverty and backwardness coupled with ignorance and lack of educational facilities. He argued the need based education for adult tribals and alternative education methods for school age children. Rebellow M. (1978) in her study found that curriculum is the main reason for high drop-out rate in tribal areas at the primary level. She suggested that the curricula should be need based keeping the local situations.

Almelu (1990) conducted a study on problems of tribal education. She found reasons such as the tribals were not willing to send their grown up children to school because they worked as labour in supplementing family income, long distance between the home and the school and in majority of the tribal areas has no transport facility to schools situated far places.

This paper is aimed to investigate the barriers of tribal pupil in retention and factors for drop-out of primary school children from schooling in a tribal Mandal.

With the above background a micro-study is conducted at Araku Mandal Primary schools of Visakhapatnam district on Barriers of Tribal Student in Pursuing Primary Education with specific objective to find out the reasons for drop-out from schools of the sample area and problem inrelation to their gender, age, parental income and family type.

Population and Sample

For the present investigation is consists 137 students selected randomly pursuing schooling and discontinued in tribal primary schools of Araku Mandal in Visakhapatnam Dist.

Area of the Problems

In the study the investigator decided to select the following problem areas in to consideration, in the aspects and they are:

1. Social problems.
2. Economic problems.
3. Infrastructural problems.
4. Teaching-learning problems.
5. Language problems.
6. Motivational problems.

There is no standard test was available the author constructed the questionnaire an after pilot study the questionnaire was canvassed personally in the field.

From the analyses the problem faced by the students in respective of Gender, Age, Class studying, Family income and family type, to enquiry the reasons for not attending the schooling are statically presented below. The specific barriers in detail are also discussed.

Distribution of the Sample

The sample consists of 137 students and majority are Male (67.2%). Regarding social sect Kondarreddy (49.6%) followed by Bagata and Valmiki sects. Majority (69.3%) from below 10 years and 38.7 per cent from above 10 years of age group. Coming to non-retention 61.3 per cent of the sample either dropped out or regularly irregular. Their parental monthly income is below Rs. 500. Students consists of 64.2 per cent and living with joint family.

The tribal students opinion were gathered on six problems they experienced in relation to their gender, age, class studying, family income and family type and presented in the following Tables 6.1 and 6.5.

Gender-wise Responses

In the tribal Students opinion towards (Area - 1) social problem theme, the boys scored higher Mean value of 1.60. The girl students Mean score is 1.3. Further, the 't' test also shows that the difference between boy and girl students is found not significantly different from each other. It shows that both the boy and girl category respondents expressed on the same opinion towards social problems.

With regard to (Area - 2) economic problems, boy students mean scores is higher than that of girl students and t test value is 2.318 which more than the table value hence it significant at 0.05 level. It shows that the both the boys and girls category respondents have different opinion towards this aspect.

Table 6.1 revels that (Area - 3) infrastructural problems are statistically significant at 0.05 level, which means boys and girl students different opinion towards this theme.

Table 6.1: Mean, Standard Deviation and 't' value for Various Gender-wise Respondents on the Themes of Opinions of Tribal Students towards Problems in Attending the Schools

Sl. No.	Area	Variables	N	Mean	SD	't' Value
1.	Area - 1	Boys	92	1.6087	1.4969	1.897
		Girls	45	1.3778	1.2301	
2.	Area - 2	Boys	92	1.8696	1.3924	2.318*
		Girls	45	1.5556	1.1192	
3.	Area - 3	Boys	92	1.9565	1.3821	2.54*
		Girls	45	1.8222	1.3364	
4.	Area - 4	Boys	92	1.8804	1.4813	2.179*
		Girls	45	1.5778	1.2521	
5.	Area - 5	Boys	92	1.8152	1.4596	2.864**
		Girls	45	2.0444	1.5515	
6.	Area - 6	Boys	92	1.6413	1.3634	2.402*
		Girls	45	2.0000	1.4924	
	Total	**Boys**	**92**	**10.7717**	**6.4826**	2.347*
		Girls	**45**	**10.3778**	**5.6901**	

In the students' opinion towards (Area - 4) teaching/ learning theme, boys scored maximum Mean value and girl Mean score is 1.57. Further, the 't' test also shows that the difference between boys and girls is found significant different from each other.

In the students opinion towards (Area - 5) language problem theme, girls Mean scores of 2.04 and boys mean score is 1.81. Further, the 't' test also shows that the difference between boys and girls students is found statically significantly different from each other.

In the students' opinion towards (Area - 6) motivational aspect, girls scored maximum Mean value and boys Mean score is 1.64. Further, the 't' test also shows that the difference between girls and boys is found significant different from each other.

The overall opinion of the students towards problems, boys mean score is 10.77 and girl score is 10.37. Further the t test value is 2.347 which is significant at 0.05 level It means that they different opinion towards the problems.

Age-wise Responses

In the tribal Students opinion towards (Area - 1) social problem theme, the below 10 years of students are scored higher mean value of 1.90. The others mean score is 0.94. Further, the 't' test also shows that the difference between below and above 10 years of age students is found significant different from each other. It shows that both the above and below 10 years of age respondents expressed on the different opinion towards social problems.

With regard to (Area - 2) economic problems, below 10 years students mean scores is higher than that of above 10 years students and t test value is 2.113 which more than the table value hence it significant at 0.05 level. It shows that the both the group respondents have different opinion towards this aspect.

Table 6.2 revels that (Area - 3) infrastructural problems are statistically significant at 0.05 level, which means below and above 10 years of age students different opinion towards this theme.

Table 6.2: Mean, Standard Deviation and 't' value for Various Age-wise Respondents on the Themes of Opinions of Tribal Students towards Problems in Attending the Schools

Sl. No.	Area	Variables	N	Mean	S D	't' Value
1.	Area - 1	Below 10 years	84	1.9048	1.4530	4.039**
		Above 10 years	53	.9434	1.1337	
2.	Area - 2	Below 10 years	84	1.9524	1.4303	2.113*
		Above 10 years	53	1.4717	1.0489	
3.	Area - 3	Below 10 years	84	2.1429	1.4574	2.539*
		Above 10 years	53	1.5472	1.1192	
4.	Area - 4	Below 10 years	84	1.9286	1.5033	1.547
		Above 10 years	53	1.5472	1.2336	
5.	Area - 5	Below 10 years	84	2.1071	1.5602	2.174*
		Above 10 years	53	1.5472	1.3092	
6.	Area - 6	Below 10 years	84	1.8690	1.4790	1.149
		Above 10 years	53	1.5849	1.2925	
	Total	**Below 10 years**	**84**	**11.9048**	**6.8611**	**3.085****
		Above 10 years	**53**	**8.6415**	**4.3857**	

In the students' opinion towards (Area - 4) teaching/ learning theme, below 10 years of age scored maximum mean value and. Further, the 't' test also shows that the difference between two groups is found not significant different.

In the students opinion towards (Area - 5) language problem theme, below 10 years of age mean scores of 2.107 and above 10 years of age mean score is 1.54. Further, the 't' test also shows that the difference between two group students is found statically significantly difference.

In the students' opinion towards (Area - 6) motivational theme, below 10 years of age scored maximum mean value and. Further, the 't' test also shows that the difference between two groups is found not significant different.

The overall opinion of the students towards problems, below 10 years of age means score is 11.9, further the t test value is 3.085 which is significant at 0.01 level. It means that they have different opinion towards the problems.

Education/Class-wise Response

In the tribal Students opinion towards (Area - 1) social problem theme, the primary students scored higher mean value of 1.75. The upper primary students mean score is 0.67. Further, the 't' test also shows that the difference between primary and upper primary students is found significant difference from each other.

With regard to (Area - 2) economic problems, primary students mean scores is higher than that of upper primary students and t test value is 3.069 which more than the table value hence it significant at 0.01 level.

Table 6.3 revels that (Area - 3) infrastructural problems are statistically not significant even at 0.05 level, which means boys and girl students have one and same opinion towards this theme.

Table 6.3: Mean, Standard Deviation and 't' value for Various Class-wise Respondents on the Themes of Opinions of Tribal Students towards Problems in Attending the Schools

Sl. No.	Area	Variables	N	Mean	SD	't' Value
1.	Area -1	Primary	109	1.7523	1.4476	3.751**
		Upper Primary	28	.6786	.8630	
2.	Area - 2	Primary	109	1.9358	1.3627	3.069**
		Upper Primary	28	1.1071	.8317	
3.	Area - 3	Primary	109	1.9541	1.4036	0.705
		Upper Primary	28	1.7500	1.2057	
4.	Area - 4	Primary	109	1.7798	1.4679	0.02
		Upper Primary	28	1.7857	1.1974	
5.	Area - 5	Primary	109	1.9633	1.4652	2.13*
		Upper Primary	28	1.6071	1.5715	
6.	Area - 6	Primary	109	1.7248	1.3735	0.561
		Upper Primary	28	1.8929	1.5715	
	Total	**Primary**	**109**	**11.1101**	**6.4698**	**2.751****
		Upper Primary	**28**	**8.8214**	**4.7769**	

In the students' opinion towards (Area - 4) teaching/ learning theme, upper primary scored maximum mean value and primary students mean score is 1.77. Further, the 't' test also shows that the difference between two groups is found not significant different.

In the students opinion towards (Area - 5) language problem theme, primary students mean scores of 1.96 and upper primary mean score is 1.60. Further, the 't' test also shows that the difference between two groups students is found statically significantly different from each other.

With regard to (Area - 6) motivational aspect, upper primary students mean scores is higher than that of primary students and t test value is 0.516 069 which more than the table value and found insignificant.

The overall opinion of the students towards problems, primary students means score is 11.11 and upper primary students score is 8.82. Further the t test value is 2.751 which is significant at 0.01 level. It means that they different opinion towards the problems.

Parental Income-wise Responses

In the tribal Students opinion towards (Area - 1) social problem theme, below Rs. 500/- pm income students scored higher mean value of 1.63. The others mean score is 1.34. Further, the 't' test also shows that the difference between two group students is found not significantly different from each other. It shows that both above and below Rs. 500/- pm income category respondents expressed on the same opinion towards social problems.

With regard to (Area - 2) economic problems, below Rs. 500/- pm income students mean scores is higher than that of counterparts and t test value is 2.57 which more than the table value hence it significant at 0.01 level. It shows that the both two group respondents have different opinion towards this aspect.

Table 6.4 revels that (Area - 3) infrastructural problems are statistically not significant even at 0.05 level, which means' both the group students have one and same opinion towards this theme.

Table 6.4: Mean, Standard Deviation and 't' value for Various Income Groups Respondents on the Themes of Opinions of Tribal Students towards Problems in Attending the Schools

Sl. No.	Area	Variables	N	Mean	SD	't' Value
1.	Area - 1	Below Rs. 500/- p.m	88	1.6364	1.4478	1.149
		Above Rs. 500/- p.m	49	1.3469	1.3471	
2.	Area - 2	Below Rs. 500/- p.m	88	1.9773	1.3644	2.57**
		Above Rs. 500/- p.m	49	1.3878	1.1331	
3.	Area - 3	Below Rs. 500/- p.m	88	1.8523	1.3437	0.69
		Above Rs. 500/- p.m	49	2.0204	1.4067	
4.	Area - 4	Below Rs. 500/- p.m	88	1.9091	1.2377	2.47*
		Above Rs. 500/- p.m	49	1.5510	1.6716	
5.	Area - 5	Below Rs. 500/- p.m	88	1.9545	1.4771	0.637
		Above Rs. 500/- p.m	49	1.7755	1.5175	
6.	Area - 6	Below Rs. 500/- p.m	88	1.9432	1.4883	2.07*
		Above Rs. 500/- p.m	49	1.4286	1.2076	
Total		Below Rs. 500/- p.m	88	11.2727	6.1152	2.01*
		Above Rs. 500/- p.m	49	9.5102	6.2952	

In the students' opinion towards (Area - 4) teaching/ learning theme, below Rs. 500/- of income scored maximum Mean value, further the 't' test also shows that the difference between the two groups is found significant different from each other.

In the students opinion towards (Area - 5) language problem theme, below Rs. 500/- PM of income scores of 1.95 and above Rs. 500/- pm of income mean score is 1.77. Further, the 't' test also shows that the difference between two groups student is found statically not significant.

Table 6.4 identify, in motivational aspect (Area - 6) are statistically significant and t value is 2.07 and the mean score of boys are higher than the girl student.

The overall opinion of the students towards problems, below Rs. 500/- pm of income mean score is 11.27, further the t test value is 2.01 which is significant at 0.05 level It means that they different opinion towards the problems.

Family Background

In the tribal Students opinion towards (Area - 1) social problem theme, below Rs. 500/- pm income students scored higher mean value of 1.63. The others mean score is 1.34. Further, the 't' test also shows that the difference between two group students is found not significantly different from each other.

With regard to (Area - 2) economic problems, joint family students mean scores is higher than that of nuclear family students and t test value is 1.351 which less than the table value hence it not significant even at 0.05 level.

Table 6.5 revels that (Area - 3) infrastructural problems are statistically significant at 0.05 level, which means joint and nuclear family students' different opinion towards this theme.

Table 6.5: Mean, Standard Deviation and 't' value for Different Types of Family Respondents on the Themes of Opinions of Tribal Students towards Problems in Attending the Schools

Sl. No.	Area	Variables	N	Mean	SD	't' Value
1.	Area - 1	Joint	70	1.7000	1.3868	1.149
		Nuclear	67	1.3582	1.4323	
2.	Area - 2	Joint	70	1.9143	1.1764	1.351
		Nuclear	67	1.6119	1.4350	
3.	Area - 3	Joint	70	2.1571	1.3581	2.176*
		Nuclear	67	1.6567	1.3320	
4.	Area - 4	Joint	70	2.1857	1.3966	3.572**
		Nuclear	67	1.3582	1.3108	
5.	Area - 5	Joint	70	2.1286	1.4736	2.932**
		Nuclear	67	1.6418	1.4740	
6.	Area - 6	Joint	70	2.0143	1.2909	2.192*
		Nuclear	67	1.4925	1.4911	
Total		**Joint**	**70**	**12.1000**	**5.1728**	**2.88****
		Nuclear	**67**	**9.1194**	**6.8568**	

In the students' opinion towards (Area - 4) teaching/ learning theme, joint family students scored maximum mean value and nuclear mean score is 1.35. Further, the 't' test also shows that the difference between two groups is found significant different.

In the students opinion towards (Area - 5) language problem theme, joint family study mean scores of 2.12 and nuclear family students mean score is 1.64. Further, the 't' test also shows that the difference between two group students is found significant.

With regard to (Area - 6) motivational problem, joint family students mean scores is higher than nuclear family students and t test value is 2.192 and significant at 0.01 level and shows difference depending on status of family environment.

The overall opinion of the students towards problems, joint family means score is 12.1 and the t test value is 2.88 which is significant at 0.01 level. It means that they different opinion towards the problems.

Major Findings

Regarding problems encountered from Social, Economical, Infrastructural, Teaching-learning process, Language and Motivational aspects are obtained from statistical analyses.

1. The overall opinion of the students towards problems, boys mean score is 10.77 and girl score is 10.37. Further the t test value is 2.347 which is significant at 0.05 level It means that they different opinion towards the problems.
2. The overall opinion of the students towards problems, below 10 years of age means score is 11.9, further the t test value is 3.085 which is significant at 0.01 level. It means that they have different opinion towards the problems.
3. The overall opinion of the students towards problems, primary students means score is 11.11 and upper primary students score is 8.82. Further the t test value is 2.751 which is significant at 0.01 level. It means that they different opinion towards the problems.

4. The overall opinion of the students towards problems, below Rs. 500/- pm of income mean score is 11.27, further the t test value is 2.01 which is significant at 0.05 level It means that they different opinion towards the problems.
5. The overall opinion of the students towards problems, joint family means score is 12.1 and the t test value is 2.88 which is significant at 0.01 level. It means that they different opinion towards the problems.

The specific barriers for drop-out among tribal children at primary level as observed from the study are as follows:

- Location of the school is far from their settlement.
- Inadequate physical facilities of the school such as *pucca* building, Lighting, seating accommodation and environmental disturbances.
- Language and curriculum in one of the reason for high drop-out.
- The formal education system is not on par with their socio-economic and cultural practices.
- The parents are not interested to send their children to schooling due to economic constrains and poverty.
- Shortage and irregularity of the teachers are also the influencing factor for discontinuation.
- The single – teacher school seems to be another factor.
- Lack of peoples participation in educating communities about need and importance of educating the children.
- The students are not attending the classes due to household work and health problems.
- Assisting the parents in food gathering and firewood, child rearing and care of the elders at home.
- Untimely supply of Text books and reading-writing material, proper dress and lack of hostel facility.
- Not coping up with other students in studies and examination.
- In sufficient grant, medium of instruction and irregular payment of scholarships and stipend.

- Non-availability of high schools in nearby place for further education.
- Parents disinterest and negligence on children education, early marriage and shifting cultivation of the parents forced the students to non-retention from the schooling.

In nutshell, both boy and girls facing some kind of barriers, while pursuing education at primary level. Boys, age below 10 years, primary class students, parental income below Rs. 500 pm and living with joint family are facing more problems than their counterparts.

Suggestions

The remedial methods suggested as per the study are, parents to be educated by non-formal method. Establishment of Residential hostels, Teaching method and Curriculum must be in tune with their socio-economic and cultural background, Language must be designed nearer to their spoken language, starting of Angnawadi's, Balawadi's and old age homes, Regular Health checkups, Regular and timely supply of reading and writing materials, Sanction of financial assistance to students, Schools must be established in congenial atmosphere with sufficient infrastructural facilities, Students parent may be encouraged by giving preference in sanctioning of Welfare schemes, Constant monitoring of administrator about school functioning and teachers regularity, Emphasis to implement and enact Child Labour laws and rules and the Educational Administrator should regularly evaluate the implementation of Right to Education and Inclusive Education programmes.

REFERENCES

Buch, M. B., Survey of Research in Education, Volumes III, IV, V.

Kalpana Kumari N., (2009), Problems of the Tribal Students in Attending the Primary Schools: A Case Study of Visakhapatnam District, Unpublished Dissertation Submitted to Mater of Education Degree to Andhra University.

Vasudeva Rao B.S., (2005), Tribal Developmental Studies (Ed. Vol.), The Associated Publishers, Ambala Cantt.

7

Tribal's and the Issue of Education

1. Dr. Vikas Mane

Tribal education is the litmus test of the social sector welfare role of the state. The tribals stay outside the urban and rural fringes and live with socio-cultural values that are distinctly different to the main stream society. Over centuries, the tribals have evolved an intricate convivial custodial mode of living. Tribals belong to their territories, which are the essence of their existence; the abode of the spirits and their dead and the source of their science, technology, way of life, their religion and culture.[1]

Our socio-culturally hierarchically stratified system made sure that the tribals stayed at the bottom of the social system and there was little accommodation and acculturation between the tribals and the rest of the social sections of the society. The tribals depended on hunting, gathering and traditional agriculture and so also remained self-reliant with their bare needs of survival. It is a cruel joke that people who can produce

1. Indian Institute of Education, Pune.

some of India's most exquisite handicrafts, who can distinguish hundreds of species of plants and animals, who can survive off forests, the lands and the streams sustainably, with no need to go to the market to buy food, are labeled as unskilled.[2] And we the mainstream, urban consider ourselves to be skilled and superior. We in the mainstream urban are superior, knowledge and skill-wise, no doubt about it. But is it superiority to attest to the highest call of development *i.e.,* sustainable development.

We, the mainstream, are pursuing the parameters of globalisation in pursuit of global material life reflecting in our education, especially higher education. We are not ready to adopt the best practices of globalisation of work culture, healthy competition, non-discrimination, equality of opportunity etc. But we are divided on caste and religion, our economy runs on croony capitalism and our education system is divided in the sciences and social sciences without employability skills and professional courses, leading to employment. On the other hand the tribals have their own guilds to learn their vocational trades without discrimination, no caste or class discrimination, no gender bias, community living and a community life conducive to sustainable development.[3]

Social exclusion describes a process by which certain groups are thoroughly disadvantaged because they are discriminated against on the basis of their ethnicity, race, religion, caste or where they live. Social exclusion is denial of the capability of individual or group to participate in, be respected by society more meaningful.

Social exclusion of children in education is an issue of violating their rights to education. Social education in education hampers the holistic development of children. The constitution of India guarantees the right of equality in education.

Literacy rate of total population and Scheduled Tribes Population and Gap in Literacy rate:

India/States/Union Territories: 1991-2001

The literacy rate in India in 1991 for the total were 52.2 and for ST's 29.6 with a literacy gap of 22.6. While in 2001 the total literacy was 64.8 the St literacy rate was 47.1 with a gap of 17.7. In Maharashtra the total literacy rate for 1991 were 64.9 with ST rate of 36.8 having a literacy rate gap of 28.1. In 2001 the total literacy rate was 76.9 with the ST rate being 55.2 having a gap of 21.7.[4]

An analysis of the socio-cultural background of the three entities global society, mainstream society and isolated tribal society is done because the three have evolved from one common platform.

Can we imagine our education system in a triad as follows:

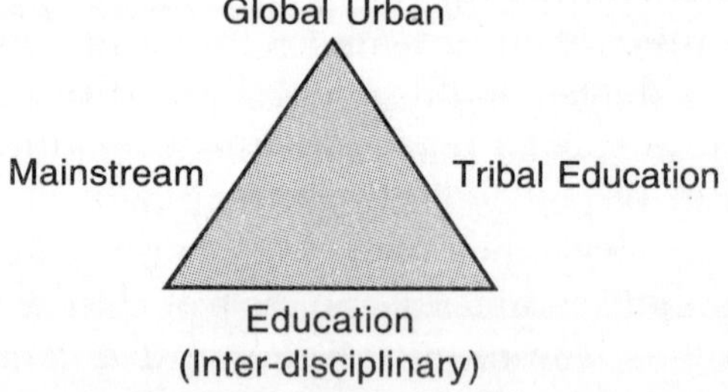

We assess the globally inspired urban mainstream educational setup on the left axis, the tribal education on the right and the two ends meeting with the best as the inter-disciplinary in education.

Now we can analyse the various parameters of education on this graph.

(a) *Separate Ashramshala:* Schools for tribal children, this concept reeks of the highest sense of patronage of the urban society on tribals. The tribals to be taught in isolation, it also reeks of a mentality of prevailing social stigmatization of the tribals. Globally cosmopolitan schools are prevailing in urban as well as in rural areas. We need the tribal children to be exposed to urban socio-cultural milieu and vice-versa. It is necessary for increased understanding, accommodation, acculturation and reduced alienated

feelings. The government of Maharashtra has recently declared on their intentions to create mixed schools. And as a bye-produce even teachers transferred to tribal schools shall not feel punished if they have to work in relative less isolated and cosmopolitan schools. Their participation of interest and convenience is an important tool of improvement in quality of tribal education.

The government in its zeal to provide facilities to the tribal's has constructed hostels for the tribal students, supplied text-books, provided different types of scholarship, etc. But instead of bridging the gap it has widened the rift.

The tribal students staying in separate hostels, availing themselves of separate scholarships, feel naturally ostracized. This should change and instead there might be some percentage reservation of seats for tribals in a general hostel and tribal students should be encouraged to take an active part in various college as well as hostel activities. Only then they could be brought into the mainstream.

(b) *Medium of Instruction:* With cosmopolitan schools instead of isolated tribal schools the issue of medium of instruction becomes tricky. But this can be solved by putting all the tribal students in one division of a class and employing a teacher who has been trained the local dialect of the tribal students or train tribal teachers for the purpose. We should create such positivism about tribal language that other non-tribal students feel like learning tribal languages the same way we appreciate tribal arts and handicrafts. It is a question of creating an environment of positivism and putting up tribal languages as the French, Italian, or Japanese languages are put up for students consumption. Then it becomes a win-win situation with the all-round understanding and acculturation on the rise.

Apart from this it has been proved that when a tribal child begins his education he starts with no linguistic information and conceptualization whereas a non-tribal child starts with a few familiar concepts and linguistics associations. So preschool training programme for the tribal child is a prime requirement and the govrnnment should undertake such programmes if it means to put the tribals on an equal footing with the non-tribal.

(c) *Teachers at School:* Lack of social mobility and the problem of inter-cultural communication are major retarding factors on tribal education. As the teacher and the taught in the tribal areas belong to different cultures the communication barrier becomes almost insurmountable.

Teachers in tribal schools are generally a more unhappy and frustrated lot. Most of the teachers appointed in tribal areas are a disinterested lot due to various problems faced by them such as lack of proper residential facility, good salary, communication facility and social distance from the tribal people. They think their posting in a tribal school is a punishment and a social stigma.[5] Sadly, officially also an errant teacher is transferred to a tribal school as a punishment posting.

It is not taken as a challenge, but a temporary unwanted destination. This attitude is a sure recipe for disaster. A disaster for the quality of education the tribal children receive. The teachers are more often not trained with the local tribal dialect.

There is simply no connect of substance between the teacher and the students. The students cannot fully understand the teachers urbane dialect and the teacher simply carry out the choirs of teaching with disinterest and even disclaim. Only greater financial incentive, quality training and cosmopolitan schools with tribals, placed in lesser isolated areas are the only solution for teachers to take greater interest in improving tribal educational quality. These are paradigm shifts and shall need great political will and greater financial provisions.

As regards appointment of teachers, more and more appointments should be made from among the tribal population so that the teachers become 'accepted' and they deal with the tribals students by using a more permissive and motivational approach.

The existing teachers should be provided with adequate facilities and they should be properly oriented. It should be a must for the teachers to learn the tribal language and there can also be attempts at writing textbooks in tribal languages.

The teacher feels isolated and unhappy and a disgruntled teacher is, certainly, not the best communicator of modern ideas and messages to tribal children. So even though the government has come up in recent times with various plans and programmes to improve the educational lot of the tribal's, there is not much result to show as there is lack of sincerity on the part of the officials charged with the implementation of these programmes. In fact a credibility gap has emerged between such officials and the tribal people. If all these problems are to be tackled successfully, the government has to bring a change in the basic orientation in tribal education.[6]

(d) *Our School:* curriculum consists of Maths, Sciences, social studies, languages and some vocational or socially useful activities with little play time. This is the same in tribal Ashram Schools notwithstanding their distinct needs and socio-cultural values.[7] What our educational system does is it gives extraordinary weight age to the sciences and mathematics. The performance of which at the secondary and higher secondary level is counted to get admission in professional and other courses leading directly to employment.

The social sciences and social studies as also other technical and vocational skills are neglected or just carried along.

The maths and sciences are abstract and technical and need to be taught well through practical's and simplified processes. The tribal teachers are simply not trained enough and motivated to do this. *Secondly,* these subjects simply do not count in the day to day life and vocational activities of the tribals. This raises the question of relevance. Relevance to a practical current and future life.

The curriculum needs to also taken in tribal activities such as agriculture, handicrafts, basic forest knowledge and medicine and mould the abundant physical energy of tribal children towards sports activities. The curriculum also needs to include modern vocations like computers and foreign languages to catch the interest and imagination through films and other educational tools and devices.

The non-tribal children should be encouraged to take up tribal art as also agriculture activities, right in the fields. This shall enthuse all children and make them value all skills and knowledge creating a kind of respect for tribal culture. This will be the foundation of quality tribal education.

(e) *Right to Education and the Tribal Children:* This is great news, especially for the tribal children. Compulsory and free education is a greater boon for the poor tribals. They shall learn in cosmopolitan schools but shall find acculturation and social acceptance difficult. But with their isolated living it shall be a challenge for the administration to spot and enroll and tribal children into schools. The tribals are also not in a position to seek redressal.

For the opponents of the neoliberal assault in education, the right to education act would make certain things constitutional – involving teachers in non-teaching work, ambiguous notion of justice vis-à-vis providing representation to 'marginalized' sections, complete neglect of issues of curriculum, pedagogy, education of the disabled children and making insufficient financial provisions.[8] The administration and schools shall have to take suo motto action to bring all tribal children into the education system. The comprehensive and continuous assessment method of evaluation shall be a greater challenge for tribal children.

This will require greater confidence, educated family background and resources to excel, what with its reliance on group activities, project making social interaction and bonding.

Ultimately our education system should be geared towards sustainable development with a virtue for excellence. For this we shall need to define the development model we shall pursue. A model based on quantity leading to massification, alienation and individual greed or one of quality leading to excellence, equitable distribution and sustainable development. We definitely have a thing or two to learn from the tribals' natural, peaceful and sustainable way of life.

NOTES

Das (Dr.) B. C. (2009), Tribal Education – Trends and Future Scenario, Regal Pubs. New Delhi.

Mohapatra S. N., Mishra B.C. (2000), Qualitative Education for Tribals – Agenda and Problems, Deep and Deep Pubs. New Delhi.

Ambasht, Nawal Kishore (1970), A Critical Study of Tribal Education, S. Chand and Co. Pubs. New Delhi.

Singh, Bhupinder, Mahanti Neeti (Ed.) (1995), Tribal Education In India, Inter-India Pubs. New Delhi.

Srinivas Nallani (2010), Tribal Education, A. P. H. Pubs. New Delhi.

D'Souza (Dr.) Nafisa Goga (2003), Empowerment and Action: Laya's Work in Tribal Education, India IEP Case Study.

Jain Seema (Vikas Samvad, Bhopal) – Tribal Struggle for Education.

Mane (Dr.) Vikas (2010), Evaluation of Secondary Level Ashramshala's in Pune District, Centre for Educational Studies, Indian Institute of Education, Pune.

Mane (Dr.) Vikas (2010), School Curriculum and Tribal Students: A Socio-Economic and Cultural Interface, Centre for Educational Studies, Indian Institute of Education, Pune.

Jain (Dr.) Ambika and Mane (Dr.) Vikas (2006), A Study of the Educational Status of the Denotified and Nomadic Tribes in Maharashtra, Centre for Educational Studies, Indian Institute of Education, Pune.

REFERENCES

1. Bijoy C. R. – 'A History of Discrimination, Conflict and Resistance, PUCL Bulletin, Feb., 2003.
2. Bijoy C.R.– 'A History of Discrimination, Conflict and Resistance, PUCL Bulletin, Feb., 2003.
3. Sah D. C. and Sisodia Y. S. (Ed) (2004), Tribal Issues in India, Rawat Pubs., New Delhi.

4. Jain Seema (Vikas Samvad, Bhopal), Tribal Struggle For Education.
5. Singh U. K. and Nayak A. K. (1997), Tribal Education, Commonwealth Pubs. New Delhi.
6. Bibhuti Mishra – Website: http;//thehindu.com/thehindu/op/2004/08/03/stories/2004080300271 3oo.htm
7. (Gare Govind-(Ed.) (1988), Maharashtrateel Adivasi Sanskriti Samasya Va Vikas, TRTI, Pune.
8. Jain Seema (Vikas Samvad, Bhopal), Tribal Struggle For Education.

8

Ashram School Teachers
Profile and Concerns

1. Dr. Jyoti Bawane

ABSTRACT

Teachers of Ashram school play a prime role in the empowerment of the tribal children, since they reside permanently in these schools. This paper presents the educational and socio-economic profile of the teachers working in Ashram Schools located in Pune district and areas for their empowerment. The study revealed that the male-female teacher's ratio was found to be disparate. Most of the teachers had rural educational background. In general, the teachers were found to be academically and professionally qualified. However, their contribution was minimal in the areas of development of teaching-learning materials, publications and participation in seminars or conferences. The socio-economic status representation of the Ashram school teachers is revealed to be more in the middle class.

1. Associate Professor, Centre for Educational Studies, Indian Institute of Education, 128/2, J. P. Naik Path, Kothrud, Pune - 411 038.

These teachers faced several challenges most those related to residential facilities, teaching-learning process and school facilities. The findings indicate that Ashram schools should recruit more female teachers, and more efforts should be made to improve their professional competence and improve infrastructural facilities of these schools.

Introduction

The scheduled tribes constitute 8.2 per cent of the total population in the country and in Maharashtra, they constitutes 8.8 per cent of the total population. India, next to Africa is considered to have the largest concentration of tribal in the world. There are over 314 tribal communities in India and who are found to live in different eco-systems. A tribe was also defined as 'a community which has a name, endogamous in nature, lives in a common territory, has a common traditional culture with an unwritten language, is structurally and culturally distinctive, relatively homogeneous, largely self-governing with no specialization of function and pervasively self-sufficient and has a conscious of ethnic identity and of belonging together (Majumdar, 1958). The literacy rate of the ST population in India is 47.10 per cent, while in the State of Maharashtra; their literacy rate is 55.21 per cent. Continuous efforts were made to improve the status of tribal students and introduction of Ashram schools was one such effort.

Ashram Schools

The tribal population largely resided in difficult terrains, access toward education was challenging to the school going children. Ashram schools as a form of educational system was introduced in early 1920's. These were residential schools located in sparsely populated areas to provide education for tribal boys and girls with free boarding and lodging facilities.

The Present Study

This study was funded by the ICSSR. The sample confined to the Ashram schools located in the District of Pune and the data was collected from 21 Ashram schools, constituting a total of 160 school teachers.

To obtain the educational and social profile of the teachers, questionnaires were administered to the selected teachers. Further, to gain insight on the working conditions, interviews were conducted with selected teachers within the given sample.

The Study Findings

The present study revealed certain alarming results which indicated need for immediate attention for the qualitative improvement of Ashram schools. Foremost is the gender representation of the teachers in these schools, which was seen that the representation of male teachers was 81 per cent, while that of the females was 19 per cent. The caste composition of these teachers was also disparate with the following proportions; general (39%), schedule caste (10.6%), schedule tribe (7.5%), vimukta tribe (3.1%) and other backward class (21.3%). In terms of religion, a majority represented Hindu (96.3%), Buddhist (2.5%), Muslim (0.6%) and Jain (0.6%). Most of these teachers received schooling in rural areas (66.9%), followed by urban (13.1%) and tribal areas (10.6%).

Looking at the educational profile of these teachers, almost half the percentage were qualified graduates (49.4%) and a relatively small percentage had qualified up to higher secondary (26.9%) and the minimum were post-graduates (19.4%). The professional qualification of the Ashram schoolteachers ranged from B.Ed to M.Phil degree. Close to half the percentage had D.Ed degrees (48.8%) and the remaining had B.Ed degree (46.3%). With regard to the kind of placement, nearly three-forths (81.9%) were appointment on regular basis, while the remaining (18%) were appointed as para-teachers.

There was a need to study the academic contributions of these teachers, in order to know their involvement in academic activities. The study results revealed that teachers' involvement in the academic activities like development of teaching-learning materials was found to be minimal. It was seen that only one-thirds (29.4%) of the teachers had developed teaching-learning materials and close to one-tenth (9%) of them had developed teacher handbooks and a negligible percentage had developed textbooks. Even Professional contribution of these teachers in terms of bringing out publications in the form of books or articles was 1.2 per cent and 4.4 per cent respectively. Nearly one-tenth (13%) participated in Seminars or Conferences or Symposiums and their participated in non-academic activities varied according to the type of the activity; sports (17.5%), cultural (16.3%), student welfare (5%) and social welfare (2.5%). Almost one-thirds of them (30%), had not attended any kind of professional training like orientation/refresher or workshops so far. The training programmes are found to be largely conducted by other agencies and less by the Zilla Parishad and Tribal Research and Training Institute.

Nearly half the percentage of teachers resided in rental accommodation (51.3%), followed by those who stayed in staff quarters (38.1%) and a minimum resided in their own house (9.4%). Since majority (81.3%) of them resided within the range of 5 km from the school, they mostly (67.5%) walked daily to school, while the rest either utilised the bus service (17.5%) or used own vehicle (13.1%) and private vehicle (1.9%).

With regard to the socio-economic profile of the ashram school teachers, their representation was maximum in middle average class (34.3%), followed by middle upper class (24.4%), middle lower class (21.3%), lower class (11.3%) and higher class (6.3%). Gender-wise there was no significant difference in the socio-economic status of male and female teachers in these schools.

Some of the concerns expressed by most of the teachers during the interviews were as follows:

1. The common problems the teachers faced were related to residential facilities, transportation, inadequate school infrastructure and classroom processes.
2. The teachers feel there was a shortage of required teaching learning materials and learning resources in the library.
3. Most of the teachers were willing to relocate to another school, preferably located close to a Taluka or city.

4. Most of the teachers faced difficulty in communicating and facilitating student participation during teaching learning process.

Discussion and Conclusion

Several disparities were noticed in Ashram school teachers' personal and educational profile, both in terms of sufficiency as well as efficiency. Most important the ratio between male and female teachers (4:1) raises concerns regarding the capability of these schools in especially retaining and facilitating the participation of the girls from the tribal community into the formal system of education. Earlier researchers drew constant attention towards the need for more female teachers in these schools, especially keeping in view that these are residential schools and more required the assistance of female teachers. (Abrol, 1988; Yadappanavar, 1990; Tyagi, 1998). There has also been a demand for more tribal teachers, to resolve the hurdle of language in these classrooms (Ambasht, 1970; Debbarman, 1992; Ananda, 2000). Teachers belonging to tribal community had advantage to have close interaction and communication with the community, as compared to non-tribal teachers (Sujata, 1992). Despite majority of the teachers in the present study obtained their education from schools located in rural areas, they also faced difficulty to relate and understand the needs of the tribal children. Heredia (1992) also advocated that Adivasi teachers would be better suited to integrate the school and community. The students found it very difficult to follow the instructions of their teachers and hence, hesitated to approach their teachers. This has resulted in the development of unfavorable attitude of the teachers towards their students (Debbarman, 1992).

The Ashram schools teachers were adequately qualified and also experienced in teaching in the selected sample. Abrol (1988) also supported this view by saying that most of the teachers were well qualified and professionally trained, with more than half being adequately experienced. However, when we look at their academic contributions, their status was not very impressive. It was believed that teachers in such a remote region found themselves isolated, stagnated and cut off from the rest of the world (Kailash, 1998) and this may be the reason for the teachers less motivation to participate in other academic activities. More attempts must be made to assess the relevance and effectiveness of the in-service training programmes conducted for the Ashram schools. This is especially keeping in view, the problems these teachers faced in their classrooms. Mathur (1992) stated that there was no common forum or in-service training arranged by the Tribal Welfare Department, so that the teachers could exchange their views and discuss their problems to widen their horizon. Financially, it does seem that these teachers had no conflicts, which was also revealed during their interviews. In general, the teachers had indicated that they were satisfied with their salaries, except for those who were appointed as para-teachers.

Most of the schools lacked basic facilities like infrastructure, furniture, water, electricity and other teaching learning materials. They ran short of teachers and classrooms; staff rooms were almost non-existent and the students of especially the lower primary class had no seating facilities. The teachers were most concerned that these students had to sit on the ground and in some schools, wooden planks or cloth spread were provided. Inadequacies in the Ashram schools or schools for ST children have been consistently revealed by earlier researchers (Mathur, 1992; Kailash, 1998; Paranjpe, 1995; Deogaonkar, 1994). Due to the above reasons, the teachers were reluctant to work in the tribal areas (Ananda, 2000; Deogaonkar, 1994) and this could be the possible reason for majority of the teachers desire to relocate to another school specifically to one located close to a Taluka or town.

Discrepancies were also noticed between the kind of problems the teachers faced and the kind of training provided to them. Hence, Need based and school specific in-service programmes are required to be introduced to enable the teachers face the challenges they faced both inside and outside the classroom. Even, training in areas that culturally orient and anthropological training with regard to cultural values and establishment rapport, etc., can be imparted to these teachers (Ambasht, 1970). Involvement of political groups was also revealed by teachers during the interviews. In most cases, their involvement was in favour of the schools while in certain cases, they were for teacher transfers and admissions. Political influence for appointment of teachers was revealed by Raskar and Surana (1989) too.

The study thus highlights that there is a need to streamline the functioning of the Ashram schools, especially in terms of the facilities to be provided for both its staff and students. Attention must also be laid to the grievances of the teachers, in order to ensure that their stress was not carried forward to their classrooms, thus affecting the classroom environments in these schools and restrain ashram school students to obtain quality education in these schools.

REFERENCES

Abrol, P. C. (1988), Constraints in the Educability of the Tribes: Gaddis, Gujjars and Bakerwals in the Jammu Region, Ph.D., Education, Punjab University. In *Fifth Survey of Research in Education*, Vol. 2, Buch, M.B. (Ed.). New Delhi: NCERT.

Ambasht, N. K. (1970), *A Critical Study of Tribal Education (with Special Reference to Ranchi District)*. New Delhi: S. Chand and Co.

Ananda, G. (2000), *Educating Tribals: An Ashram School Approach*. New Delhi: Commonwealth Publishers.

Debbarman, P. (1992), *Education among the Lepchas of Darjeeling: A Sociological Study*. New Delhi: Inter-India Publications.

Deogaonkar, S. G. (1994), *Tribal Administration and Development*. New Delhi: Concept Publishing Company.

Heredia, R. C. (1992), Tribal Education in India: The Downward Spiral. *Journal of Education and Social Change*, July-Sept. 1992, Vol. VI. No. 2. Pune: Indian Institute of Education.

Kailash, K. (1998), Tribal Schooling in Baigachak: Some Observations. *Tribal Research Bulletin*, Vol. 20 (2). Pune: Tribal Research and Training Institute.

Majumdar, D. N. (1958), *Races and Cultures of India*. Bombay: Asia Publishing House.

Mathur, P. R. G. (1992), Tribal Education in Kerala. In *Tribal Transformation in India,* Vol. 4, Chaudhuri, B. (Ed.). New Delhi: Inter-India Publications.

Paranjpe, S. (1995), Identification of Factors Affecting the Achievement of VJNT Children in Tanda Schools: A Case Study. *Journal of Education and Social Change,* Vol. 9 (3). Pune: Indian Institute of Education.

Raskar, D. M. and Surana, M.B. (1989), *Study of Working of Aided Ashram Schools Run by the Voluntary Organizations in Maharashtra State.* Pune: Tribal Research and Training Institute.

Sujatha, K. (1992), Teachers in Tribal Sub-Plan Areas in Andhra Pradesh. *Journal of Educational Planning and Administration,* Vol. 6 (4).

Tyagi, R. S. (1998), Reforming Planning and Management of School Education: A Case of Bihar. *Journal of Education and Social Change,* Vol. 12 (1). Pune: Indian Institute of Education.

Yadappanavar, A. V. (1990), *Role of Tribal Leaders in Educational Development: A Case Study in Paderu Block of Andhra Pradesh.* Pune: Tribal Research and Training Institute.

9

Some Strategies for Educational Empowerment of the Tribals in India

1. Vijay Jaiswal
2. Harish Kumar Singh

ABSTRACT

Empowerment is an active and multi-dimensional process, which enables tribal community to realise their identity and power in all aspects of life. The need for educational empowerment of tribals hardly needs justification. Their primitive way of life, economic and social backwardness, low level of literacy, out dated system of production, absence of value systems, sparse physical infrastructure in backward tribal areas and demographic quality of tribal areas make the development of tribals and tribal areas essential. Government of India has been launched a lot of programme for development of tribals. The paper disscuses some strategies for educational empowerment of tribals in India.

1. Assistant Professor (Sr.), Department of Education, C.S.J.M. University, Kanpur - 208 024.
2. Assistant Professor, B.Ed. Department, S.S. Khanna Girls' Degree College, Allahabad.

Introduction

Literally the term 'empowerment' implies 'to invest with power'. It is defined as the ability to influence the behaviour of others with or without restraint. Generally it is a socio-political process but particularly it is an individual item of self-development. It also means taking control of one's own life. In present context education is seen as the most important element for growth and prosperity of a society, of a state and of a nation. Hence, the education which invests power in somebodyelse for growth and prosperity is called educational empowerment. In other words when an individual or a body of individuals provided with such knowledge which enhances the ability for self-development or all-round development needed to lead a meaningful, dignified and civilized way of life is called educational empowerment (Barma, 2012).

Rights of the Tribal Children in India

Article 46 of the Constitution states that, "The State shall promote, with special care, the education and economic interests of the weaker sections of the people, and, in particular of the Scheduled Castes and Scheduled Tribes, and shall protect them from social injustice and all forms of social exploitation". Articles 330, 332, 335, 338 to 342 and the entire Fifth and Sixth Schedules of the Constitution deal with special provisions for implementation of the objectives set forth in Article 46. These provisions need to be fully utilised for the benefit of these weaker sections in our society.

The Constitution of India defines the *scheduled tribe* tribes or tribal communities or parts or groups within such tribes or tribal communities as are deemed under article 342 to be scheduled tribes for the purposes of the constitution. Articles 15, 16 and 17 guarantee the rights to equality as the fundamental right. Under cultural and educational rights, article 29 protects the interests of the minorities. The article reads as follows:

1. Any section of the citizen residing in the territory or any part thereof having a distinct language, scripts or culture of its own shall have the right to conserve the same.

2. No citizen shall be denied admission into any educational institution maintained by the state or receiving aid out of state funds on ground only of religion, race, caste, language or any of them.

Article 46, Part IV of Directive Principles of State policy speaks about the promotion of educational and economic interests of the Scheduled Castes, Scheduled Tribes and other weaker sections. It reads, "the state shall promote with special care the educational and economic interests of the weaker sections of the people and in particular of the scheduled castes and the scheduled tribes and shall protect them from social injustice and all form of exploitation".

The National Policy of Education was approved by the Indian Parliament in 1986. The policy gives special place to the education of the Scheduled Tribes. Besides the general policy enunciating measures and directives for the rejuvenation of education in general, it states some special measures for the education of the Scheduled Tribes.

The following measures will be taken urgently to bring the scheduled tribes (STs) on par with others.

(i) Priority will be accorded to opening primary schools in tribal areas.

(ii) The socio-cultural milieu of the STs has its distinctive characteristics including in many cases their own spoken language. This underlines the need to develop the curricula and devise instructional materials in tribal languages at the initial stages with arrangements for switching over to the regional language.

(iii) Educated and promising scheduled tribes youth will be encouraged and trained to take-up teaching in tribal areas.

(iv) Residential schools, including Ashram schools, will be established in large scale.

(v) Incentive schemes will be formulated for the scheduled tribes, keeping in view their special needs and life styles. Scholarships for higher education will emphasise

technical, professional and para professional courses. Special remedial courses and other programmes to remove psycho-social impediments will be provided to improve their performance in various courses.

(vi) Anganwadis, non-formal adult education centres, will be opened on a priority basis in areas predominantly inhabited by the scheduled tribes.

The policy has very explicitly stated that there is a need to develop curriculum and instructional materials in tribal languages at the initial stages. The distinctive characteristics of the scheduled tribes will be the basis for the development of such materials. This definitely endorses the need for making education relevant to the community. Cultural orientation of the curriculum has been a long felt need (Ambasht 1971, 2001).

Defining 'Education' in the Tribal Context

For us 'education' is an integral part of the empowerment process. Empowerment of the tribal community means capacitating tribal communities to secure access and control of their land, forest and water resources as well as sustain and promote viable alternatives for security of their livelihoods. Empowerment thus is an interactive process whereby tribal communities are enabled to participate actively in local governance (decision-making that affects their own life situation).

It is in this context that we need to define the role of adult education. For us, educating tribal communities in a more concrete sense means to facilitate processes, which will enable tribal representatives to (Laya, 2003):

- Develop an analytical capacity for assessing their external and internal environment impacting on their own communities.
- Develop confidence and capacity to articulate their interests and perspective thereby participating in decision-making processes leading to better governance.
- Develop skills to initiate local relevant alternatives to improve livelihoods and challenge external pressures.

- Value self and community history with a critical appreciation of traditional knowledge systems.

Educational Programmes in the Tribal Areas – Some Interventions

The tribal habitations are generally devoid of any other private schooling structures. In the absence of the entry of these private schools, the government schools whether they are managed by the education departments or the tribal welfare departments have to take up the challenges of educating the Scheduled Tribe children. So far, the residential Ashram schools and small schools exclusively created in the tribal habitations have been instrumental in providing schooling facilities to the tribal children. But to due to sparse population spread and inaccessible terrain habitations creating residential schools was not possible.

Some of the specific interventions being promoted for tribal children under Sarva Shiksha Aviyan (SSA) are (Panda, 2012):

- Setting up schools, education guarantee schools (EGS) and alternative schools within one km of all habitations for non-enrolled children and dropouts.
- Alternative schools provide flexibility in terms of timing, learning modalities, etc.
- Upgrading EGS schools to regular schools after two years.
- Attaching Crèches and pre-school sections *(anganwadis* and *balwadis)* to schools in tribal areas to relieve girls of sibling-care responsibilities.

Several states have relaxed the norms to set up schools – for example, in Andhra Pradesh, habitations with 20 school-age children can have a school; in Karnataka, the norm has been reduced to 15 children for an EGS school especially for tribal areas. In remote tribal habitations in the north-eastern states and Jammu and Kashmir, EGS schools can be opened with only 10 children. Andhra Pradesh has already set-up community schools in all habitations with 15 children or more,

Kerala with 20, and Madhya Pradesh with 40 children. Other innovative approaches to covering tribal children include 'contract schools', 'forest schools', summer camps, seasonal hostels, and mobile teachers. Residential ashram schools are also found in the States of Andhra Pradesh, Chhattisgarh, Kerala, Maharashtra and Odisha.

The Janshala Programme is a collaborative effort of the Government of India (GOI) and five UN agencies – UNDP, UNICEF, UNESCO, ILO and UNFPA – to provide programme support to the ongoing efforts towards achieving Universal Elementary Education (UEE). Janshala, a community based primary education programme, aims to make primary education more accessible and effective, especially for girls and children in deprived communities, marginalised groups, Scheduled Caste/Scheduled Tribes/minorities, working children and children with specific needs. A unique feature of Janshala is that it is a block-based programme with emphasis on community participation and decentralization. The blocks have been selected on the basis of different indicators such as low female literacy, incidence of child labour, and concentration of Scheduled Tribe (ST) and Scheduled Caste (SC) populations.

The interventions being promoted in States under Janshala include (Gautam, 2003):

- Schools, education guarantee centres and alternative schools in tribal habitations for non-enrolled and drop-out children.
- Text-books in the mother tongue for children at the beginning of the primary education cycle, when they do not understand the regional language. Suitably adapted curriculum and the availability of locally relevant teaching and learning materials for tribal students.
- Special training for non-tribal teachers to work in tribal areas, including knowledge of tribal dialect.
- Special support to teachers as per need.
- Deploying community teachers.
- Bridge Language Inventory for use of teachers.

- School calendars in tribal areas appropriate to local requirements and festivals.
- Anganwadis and Balwadis or crèches in each school in tribal areas so that the girls are relieved from sibling care responsibilities.
- Special plan for nomadic and migrant workers.
- Engagement of community organizers from ST communities with a focus on schooling needs of children from specific households.
- Ensuring sense of ownership of school committees by ST communities through increasing representatives of STs in VECs/PTAs etc. Involving community leaders in school management.
- Monitoring attendance and retention of children.
- Providing context specific intervention *e.g.* Ashram school, hostel, incentives etc.

The achievement of the goals for equity and inclusion in higher education would call for a strengthening of the following approaches during the 12th FYP (UGC, 2011):

(a) *Building of capacity and improvement of infrastructure* which can attract and facilitate the retention of students from rural and backward areas as well as differently-abled and marginalised social groups.

(b) Providing for pro-active measures through proper *implementation of reservation policy* for students belonging to SC/ST/OBC and the disadvantaged.

(c) *Increasing the incentives offered to differently-abled* students as well as those from the marginalised sections so that they can participate in higher education with facility.

(d) *Strengthening measures to increase the achievement capacity* of SC/ST students and those from marginalised sections so as to reduce drop-out and to improve performance.

(e) Given that a part of the gap that is observed between social groups and gender at the level of higher education is due to lower numbers and quality of passouts from

the school system due to higher drop out and segmented quality, there is a need for *improving the quality of schooling and retention of students from the marginalised sections* through enhancing the performance of the schooling cycle. The task is to be addressed by the school system.

(f) *Monitoring of performance* with respect to improving equity at the institutional level as well as higher (state and country) levels.

(g) These measures may be part of a long term plan to be drawn up to attain equity for all groups by the year 2022. This has to be drawn sector-wise with a clear roadmap.

Issues Related to Tribal Education

Some of the issues related to tribal education in India are as follows:

1. The ignorant parents and the children have poor understanding regarding the value of education.
2. Few primary schools with inadequate number of trained teachers.
3. Most of the teachers unfamiliar with the tribal language and culture fails to build rapport with the parents and the students.
4. Government funds for the development of the education are not used properly.
5. Poor class room teaching/pedagogy/methodology for joyful learning.
6. The fear of Punishment in Schools, poor quantity and quality of food, dress, reduces the interest of the students.
7. A lot of attempts have been made to mainstream the tribal children in education process. Most importantly by providing access, reading writing materials, free textbooks and empowering village community to participate in management of school. Achievements are also quite significant in areas of provision of access by opening of new schools, hostels, enrolment of children and empowerment of teachers through mass teachers training

on child centered approach. However, there seem to be lack of achievement in retention and achievement of students (on the basis of completion rates) in schools. The dropout rate is still quite high and achievement scores in subjects need significant increase (Kanungo and Mahapatra, 2004). Lack of school-related parental support, family pattern, gender roles, family insistence on the tribal child for active involvement as a labour force in the agricultural work also contribute to school dropout rate.

8. The present system of language curriculum is one of the major reasons for low educational achievements of the tribals. The dominant language of the state of Odisha, *i.e.,* Oriya, is presented as the norm or standard, value based, culturally superior, powerful and resourceful. It is also emphasised in so many ways that the tribal child must master this language in order to assimilate with the mainstream. This ultimately generates among the tribal children a feeling of inferiority towards themselves, their language, culture and their own parents and family.
9. Tribal children who go to non-tribal schools face the language problem more severely as in most cases the non-tribal classmates and teachers make fun of their mother tongue and assign low status to it. These children are forced to sit in the same class with high status Oriya children (in the state of Odisha). Usually, the teachers do not understand their language. The majority dominant Oriya language becomes a threat to the tribal children's mother tongue. It runs the risk of being displaced or replaced – a subtractive language learning situation. As a consequence, the mother tongue is not learned at all, sometimes it is forgotten and does not develop because the children are forbidden to use it, or are made to feel ashamed of it. When this happens it becomes a disastrous means of violation of linguistic human rights of the tribal children.
10. The tribal children in a tribal school do feel unmotivated to learn new non-tribal languages primarily due to

cultural differences in learning. Tribal ways of learning is through co-operation and not through modern concept of competition. Tribal culture is oral culture and not written culture (Sinha, 2005).

11. Mainstream educational institutions do not 'educate' because the curriculum does not give due consideration to the rich traditional knowledge and value systems prevalent within tribal societies These institutions do not create an opportunity to develop and learn skills which are relevant to the needs, lifestyle and aspirations of tribal communities. We believe that it is important to invest in the youth because it is they who are going to steer the future of tribal societies. Hence we have been focussing on 'alternative education' mainly with tribal youth in Andhra Pradesh (Laya, 2003).

Strategies for Educational Empowerment of Tribals in India

Education as a means of advancement of capacity, well-being and opportunity is uncontested, and more so among communities on the periphery. Marked improvements in access and to some extent in quality of primary education in tribal areas have occurred, and stem from government and non-government initiatives. However, the number of out-of-school children continues to be several millions, mainly due to a lack of interest and parental motivation, inability to understand the medium of instruction (*i.e.,* state language), teacher absenteeism and attitude, opportunity cost of time spent in school (particularly for girls), large seasonal migration etc. Low literacy rates in tribal communities continue to indicate a need for overarching support that tackles issues from health to attitudes of non-tribal populations. Education is the single most important means by which individuals and society can improve personal endowments, build capacity levels, overcome barriers, and expand opportunities for a sustained improvement in their well-being.

In the context of tribal education, finding a balance between preserving tribal cultural identity and mainstreaming for economic prosperity means building education programmes that ensure a tribal child's success in mainstream schools. Recognising that the education system is currently designed for the dominant group, there needs to be investment in creating support mechanisms that supplement the integration of tribal children into the formal education system (Bagai and Nundy, 2009).

The support within the education system includes:

- Using both tribal and state languages during the pre-primary and primary levels.
- Creating supplemental tribal relevant learning materials.
- Introducing monetary/non-monetary incentives for teachers in tribal areas.
- Addressing the health and nutritional needs of tribal children.
- Improving community participation by training tribal teachers and youth as peer educators.
- Establishing and strengthening transitional education centres which focus on mainstreaming tribal children.
- Creating seasonal hostels and residential schools for children of migratory parents.
- Training female teachers for single sex classrooms.

Kanungo and Mahapatra (2004) have suggested the following strategies for empowerment of tribal community through education:

1. Linguistic mapping should be done to assess the incidence and category of tribals before planning for their education.
2. The medium of instruction should be in the mother tongue by way of using bilingual primers prepared in a decentralized manner. That means it is not the state or district, it is the block where the teachers (tribal) with educated (although a few) tribal persons will prepare the text book for their own category of children.
3. The school environment should be attractive with gardens, plantations, and children friendly elements with cost effective locally available raw materials. The school

must have play materials and self-learning materials for the children to create interest in them to attend school regularly.

4. The teacher working in a tribal dominated school should be rightly informed about his role. He should be oriented on the richness of heritage and culture of the tribals. He should have enough patience to bear the tribal child in a classroom and act as a friend and facilitator rather than a master.
5. The non-tribal teachers working for long time inspite of various health hazards by knowing the tribal language should be identified and compensated with incentives and rewards as a token of commendations for their valuable services towards the education of tribals so that other non-tribal teachers will be interested to join the force.
6. Tribal teachers should be identified by their category and be posted to schools where he can serve his community children better.
7. The village community although illiterate, they are great assets as far as education on art and craft is concerned. Their resources should be used while topics related to agriculture, horticulture and material culture are transacted in the classroom.
8. Innovation through research on various aspects of education must be conducted so as to identify problems and their solutions.

Tribal institutions of secondary education are irrelevant and do not 'educate'. The main reason for this is that the content of education does not take into account their traditional knowledge systems, an understanding of their own environment which is rich in natural resources, relevant skills to provide access and control of their environment and a recognition of their own identity as tribal communities. Also where relevant, a major concern is the need for providing primary education in their mother tongue in order to create an opportunity for them to enhance their learning capacities.

Mainstream educational institutions tend to create an alienated group of youngsters with few opportunities to use their capacities. There is a need to review the relevance of curriculum and methodologies of education currently in the tribal context. More specifically we need to campaign for a policy, which takes into consideration the learning needs of tribal youth dropouts at the school and pre university levels (Laya, 2003).

Need to develop an informed cadre of tribal citizens in law related processes is vital. A critical understanding of the customary laws and the legal provisions in the tribal context is necessary to achieve social justice. The legal machinery in the current circumstances is either insensitive or manipulative in character.

Need to create special opportunities to respond to the educational needs of women. Consequences of the development processes are not neutral. They militate more against women than men and hence tend to result in greater negative effects on women. Loss of access and control of resources in tribal areas tend to push women out of productive activities. This also affects adversely their status in their family and community as their participation in the economy decreases. Lack of basic services, particularly related to health and education makes women especially vulnerable. Moreover, atrocities on women are on the increase, as tribal areas become accessible to outsiders and commercially oriented activities. The major strategy to address this issue is to educate the 'panchayat' representatives to safeguard the position of women in the areas under their jurisdiction (Laya, 2003).

Conclusion

Education holds the key to tribal empowerment and sustainable development. The aim of education imparted to tribals should be to bring changes not only in the amount of knowledge gained but also in the abilities to do so, to think and to acquire habits, skills and attitude which characterise an individual who is socially accepted, adjusted and economically empowered. It is unfortunate that despite sixty five years of independence, Scheduled Tribes continue to live in seclusion in difficult terrains devoid of even the basic necessities of life. Tribal development has been identified as a major field for spearheading development efforts to improve the livelihood of this particular weaker section of society by the Government of India. The success achieved in this direction has been satisfactory, but still we have to go miles away keeping in view the goal targeted in terms of socio-economic development of this vulnerable section of society in the Indian constitution.

REFERENCES

Ambasht, N. K. (1971), The Policy of Tribal Education, *Vanyajati*, Vol. XVIII, No. 1, 1971.

Ambasht, N.K. (2001), *Tribal Education, Problems and Issues*. Delhi: Venkatesh Prakashan.

Bagai, Shweta and Nundy, Neera (2009), *Tribal Education: A Fine Balance. DASRA: A Catalyst for Social Change, .www.dasra.org/n/forwebsite/dasra/.../dasrareports-tribal-education.pdf,* Accessed on Oct.13, 2012.

Barma, Padmalochan (2012), Educational Empowerment of the Tribal Women of Odisha: A Study of the PTGs of the Nuapada District of the KBK. *Odisha Review*, May, 2012, http://orissa.gov.in/e-magazine/Orissareview/2012/May/engpdf/60-65.pdf, Accessed on 02 Oct. 2012.

Gautam, Vinoba (2003), *Education of Tribal Children in India and the Issue of Medium of Instruction: A Janshala Experience*. www.sil.org/asia/ldc/parallel_papers/vinoba_gautam.pdf, Accessed on 09 Oct., 2012.

Kanungo, A. K. and Mahapatra, H. (2004), Tribal Education in Rayagada: A Review of Language, Textbook and Medium of Instruction. *Orissa Review*, Sept. 2004, http://orissa.gov.in/e-magazine/Orissareview/Sept2004/.../tribaleducation.pdf, Accessed on 09 Oct., 2012.

Laya, Nafisa Goga D'Souza, (2003), *Empowerment and Action: Laya's Work in Tribal Education, www.yerukala.info/files/misc/Laya1.pdf,* Accessed on 12 Oct., 2012.

Ibid, p. 7.

Ibid, p. 24.

Ibid, p. 25.

Panda, B. K. (2012), *Understanding Multiple Disadvantages for Inclusive Educational Development of Scheduled Tribe Children. www.ejournal.aiaer.net/vol231212/4.%20Panda%20BK.pdf,* Accessed on 10 Oct., 2012.

Sinha, Smita (2005), Linguistic Human Rights in Tribal Education in Orissa. *Language in India,* Vol. 5, 2005, http://www.languageinindia.com/may2005/smitasinhaorissa1.html, Accessed on 10 Oct., 2012.

UGC (2011), *Inclusive and Qualitative Expansion of Higher Education 12th Five-Year Plan, 2012-17.* http://www.ugc.ac.in/page/Reports.aspx, Accessed on 14 Oct., 2012.

10

Levels Educational Attainments and Enrollment Ratio of Tribal in Akkalkua Tashil of Nandurbar District

1. V. B. Bandgar
2. B. T. Nikam
3. Tele Shahaji Sopan

ABSTRACT

Education is one of the principal means of development of tribal people. Education helps to create opportunities of jobs and self-career development thus empowering male and female tribal population. It also helps to upgrade living standard with better health and assured resource of living. However it is well proved that educated tribal population present paper press into the levels of educational attainment and enrollment Ratio of tribal population in Akkalkua tashil in Nanduraba district of Maharashtra. Further it is verified encouraging and adverse factors of level of educational attainment and enrollment Ratio of the tribal population. Study is mainly based on primary and secondary source of data primary data intensive filed work. Secondary data

1. Lecturer, Uma Shikshanshastra, Mahavidyalaya Pandharpur.
2. Head and Assistant Professor, V. M. P College Natepute.
3. Lecturer, Uma Adhayapak, Vidyalaya Pandharpur.

census hand book, socio-economic Abstracts of Nandurbar districts from ongoing study it is found that the proportion educational attainments enrollment ratio in tribes in the Akkalkwa tashil selected villages at primary level, middle level, higher secondary level, state of educational attainment among the tribal is a also serious concern. Hardly 14 per cent tribal's are with primary education, less than 5 per cent S.S.C., about 6 per cent H.S.C., and graduation less than 2 per cent education at facilities are very scant only Ashramshala are made available in some villages. The literacy and educational attainment is high in those villages where Ashramshala is available. It provides hostel facility and two time meal.

Keywords: Attainment, tribal, enrollment Ratio.

Introduction

The term 'tribe' is very complex to define however it is attempted to define by considering different point of views. The constitution of Indian union (Article 366) has defended the scheduled tribe as such tribes or tribal communities as or deem under article 342 to be scheduled tribe for the purpose of constitution.

Since there are close Association of education and development of the society the role of tribal in socio-economic and cultural development of her family, society and nation is significant whom tribes are not well educated education in empowers tribes.

The present study deals with educational attainment are status of tribes in Akkakua tashil. The level of educational attainment are regarded as key variables affecting present paper aims to analysis the level of educational attainment and enrollment ratio in tribes in Akkalkua tashil.

Objectives of the Study

1. To study the level of educational Attainment for the selected villages for) for akkalkuwa tashil in Nandurbar district.

2. To study the levels of enrollment Ratio for the selected Villages for Akkalkwa tashil in Nandurbar district.

Study Region

The present study intends to assess the level of living in tribal population in Nandurbar district with reference to some selected tribal villages (Bardi, Surgas, vehgi, Biialighan, pippalkhuta) in Akkalkwa tashil of Nandurbar district in the year at Jan., 2008.

Database and Methodology

In order to meet these objective, the study is mainly based on primary data. Which have been collected by conduction by intensive field work in selected five trible villages in Akkalkuwa tashil. Researcher present study use on secondary data for the district census had book, socio-economic abstract and census of India on the information on website.

Researcher has used present study use for survey method to study this problem this is survey type of research survey method is used by researcher because the researcher works with study level of education Attainment and enrollment Ratio.

Researcher has been collecting information of educational Attainment and enrollment Ratio use for questionnaire and interview method.

Levels of Educational Attainment at Village Level

1. *Primary Education Level*: In this section the attempt is made to analyse the levels of educational attainment among tribals in 5 villages *viz*., *(i)* Surgas, *(ii)* Bardi, *(iii)* Pimpalkhuta, *(iv)* Bijaligavhan and *(v)* Vehgi. It is found that the proportion of tribal persons with primary education at village level varies from nearly 5.88 per cent in Vehgi to a maximum of 17.36 per cent in Bijaligavhan. It is a very low level of educational attainment even at primary level. It seems that where or nearby the village Ashramshala is made available, there the proportion of tribal people with primary education is relatively high than those villages where there is not. For example, the

Ashramshala was available in Bardi and Surgas and Zillah Parishad School and in Ashramshala children are provided hostel as well as food free of cost with which they are attracted to school. With this pretext they get education also. It is also noticed that male children even among the tribals are given preference over the females. In each village the Primary level educational attainment is much higher than the female children. It is important to note that the Vehgi 11 per cent males with primary education but none was among the females.

2. *Middle Educational Level*: The proportion of middle level are of 8th standard level is hardly 2 to 5 per cent in the villages of study area. The proportion of males is relatively much higher than the females. There is wide disparity between males and females at primary and middle levels.
   (i) *S.S.C. Level:* At S.S.C., level also hardly 2 to 5 per cent tribal's are 10th pass. At this ssc level, the proportion of females nowhere more than the males. The disparity between male and female is quite high.
3. *Higher Secondary Level*: At H.S.C., level or 12th standard level, it is further found that the proportion of tribal's with HSC varies between 2 and less than 6 per cent. The proportion of males that varies between 0 and about 7 per cent. So the disparity at this level is also quite high.
4. *Graduation Level*: Except Surgas, Bijaligavhan and Vehgi nowhere the proportion is even 1 per cent. And in all the cases in all the 5 villages' no single tribal women was graduate. And question of post-graduation is far away.
5. *Post-graduation Level*: At post-graduation level only in Surgas, Bardi and Vehgi where the proportion is less than 1 to 1 and 5 per cent. But none of the women are graduate and post graduate in these villages. All this very clearly indicates that where there is Ashramshala or Zillah Parishad School the proportion of tribals is relatively higher than where very high. But after HSC *i.e.*, graduation and post graduate level only very few males

Table 10.1: Nandurbar District for Akkalkuwa Tashsil Levels of Educational Attainment At Village Level Village Name

Sl. No.	Sector	Suragas			Bardi			Pimpalkhuta			Bijaligavan			Vehgi		
		T	M	F	T	M	F	T	M	F	T	M	F	T	M	F
1.	Primary (4th)	13.9	17.2	10.6	15	18.4	11.2	11.74	13.3	10	17.36	20.27	14.28	5.88	11.76	0
2.	Middle (8th)	2.63	2.98	2.27	5.39	7.63	10.4	3.17	5.45	0.66	2.77	4.05	1.42	2.94	5.88	0
3.	S.S.C. (10th)	4.51	5.22	3.78	4.04	4.86	2.78	2.53	4.24	0.66	4.16	5.4	2.85	2.94	2.94	3.03
4.	H.S.C. (12th)	5.63	6.71	4.54	2.5	3.15	1.59	4.12	7.27	0.66	2.77	5.4	0	2.94	0	6.06
5.	Graduation	1.87	3.73	0	0.77	1.380	0	0	0	0	1.38	2.7	0	1.47	2.94	0
6.	Post-graduation	0.37	0.74	0	0.77	1.38	0	0	0	0	0	0	0	1.47	0	0
	Average	5.78	7.31	4.24	5.70	7.36	5.17	4.31	6.06	2.40	5.69	7.56	3.71	3.53	4.70	1.82

Source: field survey Jan. 2008.

are going outside for higher education but females are left in the villages. This is due to geographical distance, poverty and insecurity about the female girls. If this facility of school is extended to each village within one or 2 km., distance and college near by the villages at some central point, it can enhance their levels of educational attainment which is necessary condition for their social and economic development.

Enrollment Ratio

Enrollment of children of any society reflects the development and understanding of the people regarding educational attainment. The parents who are conscious about education of their children, they make it tangible at any cost to send them to school. This is truer in case of higher caste children particularly of Brahmins. But nowadays the other people (other than the Brahmins) have also understood the importance of education but their poverty, illiteracy, some social problems entail them to withdraw, their children from school and in such a case the drop out rate is quite high. For example, the enrollment ratio varies from 35.29 per cent in Vehgi to near about 60 per cent in Bardi. On an average more the 40 per cent children are not being enrolled even at primary level. On an average 45 per cent children are not being enrolled this may be because of geographical of 6-10 age groups all should get enrolled in the school but it has not happened even in 2008.

1. *Higher Primary Level*: At higher primary level, in Vehgi and Bijaligavhan hardly 1/3 of the children between 11 and 14 are being enrolled and in Bardi nearly 59 per cent, Surgas 66 per cent and Pimpalkhuta 79 per cent. On an average 46 per cent children remain outside the school. At secondary level nearly 48 per cent children of 15 to 16 age group are attending the school.
2. *Secondary Level:* At secondary level, the enrollment has declined from 54 per cent at higher primary to hardly 44 per cent at secondary level. The minimum enrollment was 25 per cent in Vehgi village and the maximum was 70 per

cent in Pimpalkhuta. This decline is due to non availability of the secondary schools within the reachable distance. Moreover the communication system is very poor.

3. *Higher Secondary Level*: At higher secondary level also the enrollment is hardly 43 per cent. It is very surprising to note that none was enrolled for higher secondary level of education. But in Surgas village where Ashramshala was available which provide food and accommodation to the students who were enrolled. The enrollment was as high as 87 per cent, whereas in Bardi it was 20 per cent. The disparities in enrollment are very sharp. This high percentage of enrollment at higher secondary level in Surgas village, in Bijali gavhan and Pimpalkhuta is because of the accumulation of failure students. High percentage does not mean that enrollment has increased.
4. *Graduation Level*: At Graduation level, on an average the enrollment is hardly 5 per cent and 95 per cent dropout. In Vehgi and Bijaligavhan none was enrolled for graduation. It was only in Bardi, Surgas and Pimpalkhuta where a few were enrolled for it otherwise the condition after higher secondary is serious one. Neither the facility nor their economic condition allows to get enrolled.
5. *Post-graduation Level:* Hardly 1 per cent that is too in Surgas village, tribals were enrolled for post-graduation who must have been taking education outside the village otherwise except Surgas nowhere any person was found enrolled for post-graduation. As a whole, it is infened that until unless they will attain higher level of education, heir living condition cannot be improved.

Conclusion

It is inferred that the tribal literacy has increased 36.79 per cent to 55.20 per cent in 1991 and 2001. Similarly, rural literacy from 32.67 per cent to 55.30 per cent and urban 64.58 per cent to 74.20 per cent. The female literacy has been increasing at a bit faster rate. Male-female as well as rural-

Table 10.2: Akkalkuwa Tashsil Nandurbar District Enrollment Ratio At Village Level

Sl. No.	Education	Primary	M.P	Secondry	H.S	Gradution	P.G
		I-IV	V-VII	VIII-X	XI-XII	XIII-XV	X-VI-XVII
	Age Group	6 to 10	11 to 14	15 to 18	17 to 18	19 to 21	22 to 24
	Village Name						
1.	Bard	69.9	58.75	40	20	8.57	0
2.	Surgas	63.15	65.71	47.61	88.66	12.5	5
3.	Vergi	35.29	33.33	25	0	0	0
4.	Bijaliga Han	48.38	33.33	35.71	55.55	0	0
5.	Pimp Alkhuta	60	79.16	70	53.33	4.54	0
	Average	53.34	54.65	43.66	43.1	5.12	1

Source: fielcwork Jan. 2008.

urban disparities among the tribes have also been declined in the state of Maharashtra. The disparity between tribals and non-tribals has been reduced from 0.323 in 1991 to 0.232 in 2001.

At village level the male-female disparity is very high. The overall male-female literacy rates are also quite low because of poverty and very poor communication system. The enrollment rate at primary level is about 54 per cent, which comes down to 43 per cent at higher secondary level and at graduation level is just 5 per cent. The dropout rate is very high. The educational attainment among the tribes at primary level is hardly 13 per cent, at middle 2.6 per cent, at S.S.C. 4.5 per cent, at H.S.C. 5.6 per cent and at graduation 1.88 per cent, The educational attainment after primary is almost negligible. This is all due to their absolute poverty, unemployment, poor roads and communication system, non-availability of schools in the villages, social insecurity for girls, etc., are some of the reasons of their low literacy, high male, female disparity and high dropout ratio. It can be improved by increasing their purchasing power by improved by increasing their purchasing power by providing employment medical services and other attention needs for raising their living standards.

REFERENCES

Bapuji, M. (1993), "Tribal Development Administration", Kanishka Publishing House, Delhi.

Black, 'Maggie (2005), International Development, Rawat Publications Jaipur.

Choudhari, Buddhadeb (1985), Tribal Health: Socio-cultural Dimension", Inter-India Publication, New Delhi.

Dandekar and Rath (1974), Poverty in India, School of Political Economy.

Kulkarni, A. D. (1991), Tribal Education Problems and Prospects.

Thapar, Ramesh (1977), Tribe, Caste and Reguigion in India", Macmillan India Ltd. Delhi.

Ramotra, K. C. (2008), Development Processes and the Scheduled Castes Rawat Publication Jaipur.

Swamy, R. N. (2011), University News.

11

Difficulties of Tribal Education in India

1. Arjunan. M
2. Dr. M. Balamurugan

Introduction

The constitution of India, under article 366, has defined as scheduled tribes, of those Tribes or tribal communities which have been so declared by the constitutional order article 342 for the purpose of the constitution. There are 574 tribal groups who have been identified as scheduled tribes. They have been previously described as aborigines, aboriginals, primitives, adivasis, vana jatis etc., special provisions have been made in article 46, 275, 330, 332, 335, 338, 340 etc., to safeguard the interests of scheduled tribes and to protect them from social injustice and exploitation. One of their distinguishing features is that majority of them live in scattered and small habitations located in remote and inaccessible settlements in hilly and forest areas of the country. Most of the tribal-concentrated

1. Ph.D Scholar, School of Education, Pondicherry University, Puducherry - 605 014.
2. Associate Professor, School of Education, Pondicherry University, Puducherry - 605 014.

areas lack of basic facilities such as roads, transport, communications, electricity, medical facilities etc., the literacy rate among tribes is low, but also varies widely among different groups and regions. More importantly, a considerable portion of tribal children continue to be outside the school system.

Government planners see education an indispensable for helping tribal peoples cope with national integration. Education will also determine their prosperity, success and security in life. The tribes which remain either deprived of or negligent toward education will suffer the consequence. Tribal youths also feel that teachers endeavor to undermine the attitudes toward their own customs, mannerisms, language or toward their cultural heritage in general.

Problems among Tribal Education People

Often both physically and socially isolated from communities, scheduled tribes have lower enrolment and achievement rates and higher dropout rates than the non-tribes. The major causes for the gap in education field of tribal education, to mention a few, are cultural discontinuity between family and school, the language of instruction and quality of schools. In tribal communities, most of the children are first generation.

Economic Problems

It is a fact that poor economic condition is one of the main problems of backwardness in education of the tribes. Most of tribes' occupation is agriculture in the peak season, they require extra hands for help in agriculture operation as well as earned money and as a result, boys and girls remain engaged in this work. Therefore, they discontinue their study for the sake of plantation and harvesting. Instead, the parents have to feed the child out of their earning which further reduces the economic stability of the family. Thus, they are the assets of family, otherwise they will be liabilities.

Socio-cultural Problems

The socio-cultural problems are more complicated than the economic problem. Tribal people have attachment towards their age old socio-cultural traditions. The parents shows the little interest of their male children than the female children move here and there, play the rural traditional games in the lap of nature and swim during mid day in village pond or stream in rainy season. The activities of the tribal children are entwined with their family and society. In the tribal societies early marriage is one of the hindrances to education. Primary and middle schools are situated in and around the tribal area but In most of the cases the high schools are located far from villages. As a result large number of girl students discontinues their education after primary or middle level.

Psycho-social Problems

The Tribal children are of wandering nature, shy and have least interested in education. Even in few cases the school going children face some adjustment problems with non tribal students. In the context psychological clash has also a greater role in the educational development. Even unemployment factor also discourage them in getting educated.

Environmental Problems

There is no sustainable physical home environment for development of formal education among the studied tribal groups. Most of tribal people using drunk for this purpose they spend a part of amount of earned money and it directly effects the economy of family as well as their children's education badly. In tribal area there is no sufficient light facility that's why they taking early dinner and going to bed early as they are engaged in hard work from dawn to dusk and feel very tired in the evening. In some cases, non-availability of schools at approachable distance and schools in the dilapidated building with inadequate number of essential furniture's has also been found. In this context teacher regularly faces many problems in classes.

Teacher and Teaching

The successful implementation of the programmes of education depends on quality of teachers. In tribal areas, school teacher are non tribes they come to the school from distant places on foot or bicycles. Naturally most of them are late comers and they like to take complete rest during the classes. The outside teachers generally take the leave frequently during the rainy season. They never try to motivate the parents of tribal children about the importance of education of their children. So, suitable teachers and a new education policy are essential to spread the education among the tribes.

Medium of Instruction

Language is one of the major problems to tribal education. In general, Tribal languages and dialects are in rudimentary stage. Again the school teachers are non-tribal outsiders and they have no or less idea about tribal languages and culture. It is an acceptable fact that language problem is also a prime barrier in educational development of the tribes. The medium of instruction plays a vital role in understanding the subject matter.

Policies for Development of Tribal People

For the first time after the country became independent, the government of India is proposing the formulation of a national policy on scheduled tribes. The policy seeks to bring scheduled tribes into the mainstream of society through a multipronged approach for their all-round development without disturbing their distinct culture.

The constitution through several articles has provided for the socio-economic development and empowerment of scheduled tribes. But there has been no national policy, which could have helped translate the constitutional provisions into a reality. Five principles spelt out in 1952, known as Nehruvian Panchasheel, and have been guiding the administration of tribal affairs. They are:

1. Tribals should be allowed to develop according to their own genius.
2. Tribals rights in land and forest should be respected.
3. Tribal teams should be trained to undertake administration and development without too many outsiders being inducted.

4. Tribal development should be undertaken without disturbing tribal social and cultural institutions.
5. The Index of Tribal development should be the quality of their life and not the money spent.

The new education policy was formulated in the year 1986. It has accorded high importance to education of scheduled tribes, particularly to the Universalisation of elementary education. The main purpose is laid on micro-level planning taking family as a unit. Non-formal education was suggested for school children of 9-14 years of age groups. The Acharya Ramamurti Committee which reviewed this National Educational Policy of 1986, strongly recommended that education should be made socially relevant and meaningful because this education policy is more socially relevant along with core curriculum, establishment of school complex, providing additional teachers to the single teacher school., opening of hostels in every district, identifying teachers from educated tribes, expanding ashram schools, providing pre-primary education and paying opportunity cost or some of the important schemes found in the Programme of Action (POA). Moreover, it may be stated that the national policy on education, 1986 envisages decentralized and micro-level planning in order to cater to the local educational needs.

Conclusion

India is one of the countries having largest number of population in the world having highest percentage of dropout at higher primary level because of poverty and over population. The tribes of this country are having fascinating rich cultural heritage and played a significant role in enrichment of composite culture. Have been identified as less acculturated tribes among the tribal population groups and in need of special programmes for their sustainable development, the tribes are awakening and demanding their rights for special reservation quota for them.

People should develop along the lines of their genius and should avoid imposing anything on them. We should try to encourage in every way their own traditional arts and culture. We should try to train and build up a team of their own people to do the work of administration and development. Some technical personnel from outside will no doubt be needed, especially in the beginning. But we should avoid introducing too many outsiders in to tribal territory. We should judge results, not by statistics or the amount of money spent, but the quality of human character that is evolved.

REFERENCES

Bhandari J. S. and Subhadra Mitra Channa (1997), *Tribes and Government Policies*, Cosmo Publications, New Delhi.

Midatala Rani (200), *Problems of Tribal Education in India*, Kanishka Publishers and Distributors. New Delhi.

Manmatha Kundu (1994), *Tribal Education New Perspectives*, Gyan Publishing House, New Delhi.

Nabakumar Duary (2010), *Education in Tribal India*, A Mittal Publication, New Delhi.

National Curriculum Framework 2005, *Problem of Scheduled Caste and Scheduled Tribe Children*, National Council of Educational Research and Training, New Delhi.

Sujatha K. (1999), *A Study of Community Schools in the District of Vishakhapatnam*, Andhra Pradesh, International Institute for Educational Planning/UNESCO.

12

Elementary Education of Tribal Children in Government and Private Schools

Question of Accessibility, Affordability and Acceptability

1. Dr. Sambit Kumar Padhi

ABSTRACT

India being a classic home land of scheduled tribes, offers a very sound human laboratory for conducting a number of researches. The diverse issues of scheduled tribes in general and their educational development in particular received a wide attention among the researchers since a long time because time has tested that education is an inevitable force for the holistic development of people and nation. Since Independence several commissions and committees were set up to assess the progress of tribal education and with an objective to mainstreaming the tribals. A close analysis reveals that literacy and enrolment of tribal children are quite gloomy and considerably lower than the other category of students. Realising the importance of education, in 2009, Government of India enacted the Right to Education

1. Assistant Professor, Department of Education, Guru Ghasidas Vishwavidyalaya, Bilaspur, Chhattisgarh. E-mail: padhiggv@gmail.com.

Act (RTE) that defines elementary education as a fundamental right of every Indian child. In these circumstances, it is pertinent to assess how far the present education system has succeeded in providing quality elementary education to scheduled tribe children, who suffers the double discrimination of non-accessibility and non-acceptability sociologically, psychologically and geographically. Researches also reveal that most of the tribals are fatalistic past oriented, survival minded and have narrow economic horizon. Their self-concept is low and locus of control is externally situated as they depend much on external authority for guidance and support. Keeping all the above points into consideration, the paper highlights briefly about the tribal in Indian context, *i.e.*, socio-economic and geographical features, population, etc., in the first part. The second part examines the enrolment, drop-outs, attendance of tribal students in elementary level comparison to other category of students. The third part deals with specific problems of tribal children and finally attempts has been taken to provide some measures to close the gap.

The scheduled tribes constitute the most backward among the weaker and disadvantaged sections in India. The social reality of 'ADIVASI' in post colonial India is characterised by poverty, malnutrition, illiteracy, socio-economic and sexual exploitation by settlers and the depletion of their traditional base. The study of Indian tribe has impressed many researchers for a long time. Being a classic home land of scheduled tribes India constitutes about 8.2 per cent of tribal population of the total population. There are near about 645 tribal groups scattered in all most all states of India. Their contribution in shaping Indian culture through their language, tradition, customs, and integrated worldview cannot be ignored. Their rich cultural and human value system contains the powers to maintain the cultural bio-diversity thereby keeping the globe ecologically sound. But unfortunately they are under-estimated, misjudged and historically marginalized. Their land, culture and heritage, which are established in more eco-

socio-religious life through oral tradition are yet to be recognised in the modern educational domain. Historically, some token measures have been taken to incorporate their languages and cultures in the mainstream school education, but nowhere in the country, till today, has a culturally appropriate curriculum for the tribal children ever been made to ensure linguistic and cultural right that enshrined under Article 46 of the Indian constitution.

Education for Scheduled Tribe

Education is the mirror of the society and is the seed as well as flower of the socio-economic development. It transcends human being from ignorance to enlightment, from shade of social backwardness to the light of social amelioration and the nation from under development towards faster social and economic development.

Realising the importance of education for a large, democratic and welfare country like India, Indian constitution enshrines certain provisions promising equality of educational opportunities for all. In pursuance of these provisions, State and Central Government have given wide attention for promotion of education among all categories of socially and culturally disadvantaged groups in general and tribal students in particular. Despite of incentives and special care for the development of education amongst the tribes, the process of educational development has far from satisfactory.

Constitutional Provision

Constitution of India article 29 (1) and Article 350 (A) safeguard the linguistic right of the minority children in school. It is the duty of the state to provide education to the children of linguistic minority children in the school at least in the primary stage.

- *Article 21 A*: Free and compulsory elementary education of equitable quality for all children up to 14 years of age.
- *Article 29 (1)*: Any section of the citizens residing in the territory of India or any part there of having a distinct language, script or culture of its own shall have the right to conserve the same.

- *Article 46*: States to promote the Educational needs of the weaker sections of the society.
- *Article 350A*: It shall be the endeavour of every State and of every local authority within the State to provide adequate facilities for instruction in the mother-tongue at the primary stage of education to children belonging to linguistic minority groups; and the President may issue such directions to any State as the considers necessary or proper for securing the provision of such facilities.

In addition to the above mentioned constitutional provisions, all most all the committees and commissions emphasised on the tribal education time to time.

The National Policy on Education, 1986 and Modifications of 1992

The National Policy on Education was formulated in 1986 and was slightly modified in 1992. The Fourth Chapter of this document has been entitled as 'Education for Equality' where in the education of the scheduled Tribes has been spelt out in detail. These are:

(i) Priority will be accorded to opening primary schools in tribal areas. The construction of school buildings will be undertaken in these areas on a priority basis.

(ii) The socio-cultural milieu of the Scheduled Tribes has its distinctive characteristics including, in many cases, their own spoken languages. This underlines the need to develop the curricula and devise instructional materials in tribal languages at the initial stages, with arrangements for switching over to the regional languages.

(iii) Educated and promising Scheduled Tribe youths will be encouraged and trained to take up teaching in tribal areas.

(iv) Residential schools, including Ashram Schools, will be established on a large scale.

(v) Incentive schemes will be formulated for the Scheduled Tribes keeping in view their special needs and life styles. Scholarships for higher education will emphasise

technical, professional and para-professional courses. Special remedial courses and other programmes to remove psycho-social impediments will be provided to improve their performance in various courses.

(vi) Anganwadis, non-formal and Adult-Education Centres will be opened on a priority basis in areas predominantly inhabited by the Scheduled Tribes.

(vii) The curriculum at all stages of education will be designed to create an awareness of the rich cultural identity of the tribal people as also of their enormous creative talent.

The Modifications of 1992 did not contain any significant changes in the policy prospective relating to tribal education. In the 1986 Policy, it was envisaged that the normal funds for education, as well as under the NREP, RLEGP, Tribal Welfare Scheme etc., should be utilised to open primary schools in tribal areas. In the 1992 modification the Jawahar Rojgar Yojana was substituted for NREP and RLEGP.

Elementary Education

India has the dubicious distinction of having one of the largest elementary education systems in the world. With more than 15 crore children enrolled and having more than 30 lakhs teachers, the elementary education is expending in the country in a significant scale. The literacy rate of the country has been increased from meager 18.33 per cent in 1951 to 65.38 in 2001. In reiterating it stands for universalisation of primary education in the country, the 86th amendment to the constitution of India has made free and compulsory education to the children of 6-14 age groups as a fundamental right.

The government of India has launched several educational programmes for all categories of student in general and tribal students in particular after independence, more recently, the government of India has launched Sarva Shiksha Abhiyan (SSA), a flagship programme (2001) in partnership with the state government to cover the entire country. In addition to this, Right to Education Act came into effect on April 2010, with an objective to provide free and compulsory education to every child up to the eighth standard, irrespective of class and gender. Analysis reveals that there is no such eye catching improvement has been occurred among the tribal students in elementary education.

Literacy is an important and primary index of educational development. This section provides data on the position of literacy among the tribals with reference to literacy of total population.

Table 12.1: Literacy Rate among Total and ST Population of India by Sex (in %)

Census Year	Total Population			ST Population			Gap between ST and Total Population
	Male	Female	Total	Male	Female	Total	
1961	37.16	15.34	28.31	13.04	2.89	7.99	20.32
1971	45.95	21.97	34.45	17.09	4.58	10.89	23.56
1981	56.37	29.75	43.56	24.52	8.04	16.35	27.21
1991	63.86	34.42	52.11	40.65	18.19	29.60	22.51
2001	75.26	53.90	64.84	59.17	34.76	47.10	17.74
2011	82.1	65.5	74.0	NA	NA	NA	——

* Census of India, 1961-2011.

Data of Table 12.1 reveals that tribal literacy was 7.99 in 1961 and it reached to 47.10 by the year 2001. As per 2001 census the total literacy rate of the tribals in India is 47.1 per cent where as it is 64.84 per cent at the national level. And on the basis of male-female percentage, the tribal male accounts 59.17 per cent (75.26 national) and female 34.76 per cent (53.9 national). According to 2001 census, ST population of India have the lowest level of literacy followed by the SC of the country. Analysis indicates that there is a safe gap between the tribal and overall literacy both in state and central level. Even today tribal literacy falls well below the national average. Besides this, disparity among various states in terms of tribal literacy rates is pretty high.

Table 12.2: Enrolment of Total and ST Students in Elementary Schools in India by Sex (I-VIII)

Year	General All Category Students			ST Students		
	Boys	Girls	Total	Boys	Girls	Total
2005-06	99391598	84982281	184373879	10033028	8616990	18650018
2006-07	100940969	91255049	188196018	10241811	8851120	19092931
2007-08	102139988	90535277	192675265	10270502	9128038	19398540
2008-09	99510768	90519505	190030273	10670945	9648194	20319139
2009-10	102673283	92417562	195090845	10624683	9640233	20264916

*SES.

Table 12.3: Gross Enrolment Ratio of Total and ST Students in Elementary School in India by Sex (I-VIII)

Year	General All Category Student			ST Students		
	Boys	Girls	Total	Boys	Girls	Total
2005-06	98.50	91.05	189.67	111.98	101.34	106.76
2006-07	100.43	93.47	97.08	114.71	104.16	109.57
2007-08	102.36	98.02	100.28	116.26	108.94	112.70
2008-09	100.45	99.09	99.80	122.00	116.64	119.39
2009-10	103.75	101.09	102.47	121.14	116.41	118.85

*SES.

Table 12.2 and 12.3 shown that elementary school enrolment and gross enrolment ratio of tribal students in comparison to all category of students from 2005-06 to 2009-10. A close observation indicates that both the enrolment and gross enrolment of tribal students have been increased from 2005-06 to 2009-10 but the growth is quite non liner. Total enrolment of tribal students in the year 2005-06 was 18650018. During subsequent years, it increased and by the year 2009-10 it was 20264916. It also indicates that gross enrolment of tribal students have been rising year by year. Although there is a overall growth of enrolment of tribal students year by year but it is quite law with reference to National Enrolment.

Table 12.4: Drop-out Rate of Total and ST Students in Elementary School in India by Sex (I-VIII)

Year	General All Category Student			ST Students		
	Boys	Girls	Total	Boys	Girls	Total
2005-06	48.49	48.98	48.71	62.76	33.20	62.95
2006-07	46.44	45.22	45.90	62.78	62.22	62.54
2007-08	43.72	41.34	42.68	62.62	62.31	62.48
2008-09	44.89	38.86	42.25	57.66	58.99	58.26
2009-10	40.59	44.39	42.39	55.15	60.64	57.78

*SES.

Table 12.4 shown drop-out rate of total and tribal students in elementary school. A close observation indicates that drop-out rate of tribal students have been decreased from 2005-06 to 2009-10. So far the year wise analysis is concerned it was 62.95 in 2005-06 and reduced to 57.78 by the year 2009-10. In case all categories of students it was 48.49 in 2005-06 and reached to 40.59 by the year 2009-10. It indicates that drop-out rates has been decreased in both the categories of students and overall drop-out rates of tribal students year by year is quite high in comparison to National average.

Question of Accessibility

At present school education of all most all the states are offered through dual mode. One segment comprising private institutions catering to the affluent near about 5 per cent of the population and the second consisting of low quality institutions meant for the masses. In other way, very few per cent of students enrolled in private schools and most of the tribal students are enrolled in state government schools. Researches reveal that state has put very little effort towards equitable distribution of quality education meant for the masses. The principles of equity and access have been exercised into maximum extent in government schools but matter of great questions in private institutions. A close observation reveals that private schools are reluctant to give admission to the tribal children even though RTE Act made a provision of

25 per cent seats reservation for children from disadvantaged community.

The study of Sam Mohanlal (2001) highlights that main reason for dropout is the total incompatibility between the students and the use of language in the text books, language used by the teachers in the school, and the content of the text that are not eco-friendly. Despite several policy recommendations and constitutional provision (article 350 A) of mother tongue for linguistic minorities at primary level, in practice there is no education in tribal language (Nambissan 2000). Many researches pointed out that non-tribal teachers tend to see home language of tribal children is one of the barriers for tribal children.

So far academic performance of tribal students are concerned, it is found that they are poor in studies because they could not grasp the matters easily, do not get tuitions and are usually first generation learners. Impoverished home environment do not provide money, time, facilities, support, guidance and motivation for their studies and this led tribal students to remain quiet, secluded, passive, non-participative and uninvolved in school. Also, they seldom receive any support from the school for the development of a positive sense of self. Almost all the studies in this regard in India showed that the tribal students in primary classes have lower achievement scores compared to non-tribal population Shukla, (1994), Govinda and Varghese, (19890, Jhangira (1993), Varghese (1993), Sujatha, (1998), Prakash, (1998). The low achievement levels among tribals were attributed to school related variables as in the case of non-tribal students. However, the tribal students had additional disadvantages arising out of social and location factors that affect their achievements levels. In other words the tribal students' performance varies among different schools irrespective of their location, family background and management type of the school (Sujatha, 1998).

With the change of society, tribal students have slowly been getting awareness about educational facilities. But the factors like distance of schools from their home, road connectivity and economic compulsion do not allow them to make use of such available facilities. Most of the teachers are not comfortable with tribal dialect and teaching learning materials are not available as per their understanding due to which tribal students have developed negative attitude towards the school and teachers.

It is also seen that intensity of in service training programme for teachers of tribal schools was not so prominent. In order to minimize the problems, the state government should make efforts to fill up the adequately number of tribal teachers with proper qualification.

Question of Affordability

Tribal communities are well known for their backwardness, poverty and ignorance. Most of the tribal population have a law economic profile. A study of Krishnan pointed out that social and economic condition of tribal community is the major factor of low educational achievements and low aspiration of tribal students. Result of his study revealed that tribal children live in unhealthy environment, do low paid physical labour and own very little land. Providing education to the children in private schools is almost a difficult task for tribal parents due to high admission fees and other expenses and getting education in private schools is almost a laborious task for tribal students in terms of maintaining the speed of learning, quality of text materials and meeting the expectation of teachers.

Problems of Acceptability

Tribals are usually poor, illiterate and superstitious. Most of them are conservative and primitive in their outlooks. They do have a belief that present system of education will no way help to their children and will diffuse their customs and traditions. It will not provide any immediate gain to their children. Normally the tribals ignore the education at the initial stage of life and reluctant to send their children to outside for education. On account of ignorance and social traditions, tribals normally do not accept any new interventions in their life styles in general and education in particular. Therefore they do not avail themselves of educational facilities scattered in and around their locality.

The issue that emerges from the various studies is that tribal children continued to be 'back benchers, poor achiever, inferior in comparison to other students of the schools and society. Discrimination existed not only at the level of curriculum, but also at the behaviour and pre conceived notions and attitudes of teachers that were equally responsible for existing disparities. Classroom transaction was based on conventional pedagogy of teaching *i.e.,* limited to text books and rote memorization. Conventional pedagogy and teacher's attitude compelled these students to being way from the class mentally as well as physically. All these factors thereby influenced the development of self-confidence, character, and personality that lead to poor performance and unsatisfactory education growth.

It is observed that tribal children hesitate to communicate with their teachers and non-tribal counter parts because they feel that they are not competent enough and develop a kind of inferiority. Negative impression of teachers and peers generates a determinal impact on tribal students perception making them develop poor self-confidence and discouraging them to reach the goals set by the teachers and others.

The studies of Sharma (1979), Patel (1985), Menon (1987), Ali (1988), Das Gupta (1988), Chaudhari (1990) and Basu (1990 and 1992) on different tribes across the country highlighted as to what extent the social beliefs, customs, ecological imbalances and external interventions have adversely affected the economic and demographic profiles of the tribes in general and their health, sanitation and education in particular.

Thus, there is a need to address the critical role that culture plays in education of tribal children. Mother tongue in the early stages will no doubt build the child's potential and self-confidence. Teachers need to be sensitized in the teacher education programme about the marginalized and disadvantaged groups, their culture and languages and home-school linkages in order to tackle the ongoing and upcoming problems related to their education.

Conclusion

Tribal community is skilled in many aspects. In order to meet the local requirement they never depend upon the outside market. They fulfill their day to day requirements with the help of natural resourses. In the modern society, most of their skills are found unrecognised and their skills and potentialities are found unappreciated. In order to make them self-employment and to enhance the economic condition of the tribal family, necessary orientation for improving the various skills needs to be taken-up.

Although a few tribal students do benefit from education in present time, they represent cream of the community and not the masses. In this connection, educational management should be decentralized in tribal areas considering the geographical terrain and the communication problems of tribal students.

From the above study it can be concluded that present education system for scheduled Tribe is not well planned one. Even though government has succeeded in the enrolment level but overall education system more or less has failed to meet the needs of tribal students. A close observation indicates that there is seasonal absenteeism or non-attendance by the tribal students in the age group of 6-14. Attendance in the schools is low during the period from December to April than the period from august to November. During the former period must of the tribal rituals and festivals are observed which impel some of the students to stay back at home, and during the later period there is general scarcity of food at home. Lack of motivation, awareness, economic condition of parents, shortage of trained teachers, reading materials, poor infrastructure facilities etc., are the primary causes behind this. Above all various programmes like orientation programmes, sensitization programmes should be organized for tribal community to reduce the non-enrolment, non-attendance and drop-outs of tribal children.

A time has come to do something serious about the educational empowerment of the tribes in general and primitive tribes in particular. Government alone cannot do this. It needs a concerted and continuous effort by the Government, non-Government organizations and corporate groups. The effective public-private partnership (PPP) can solve the problem to many contexts. If all the agencies and groups come forward with innovative ideas to educate the tribes with a suitable and amicable environment then after a decade or two the next generation tribes will take over and take care of their state as well as of their motherland.

REFERENCES

Annamalai, E. (2001), Managing Multi-culturalism in India: Political and Linguistic Manifestation, New Delhi: Sage.

Das Gupta, N. K. (1959), Tribal Language and Education, Man in India.

Department of Education (1968), National Policy on Education. Ministry of Human Resource Development, Government of India, New Delhi.

Dubey, S. C. (1972), Expert Committee on Tribal Development, GOI, New Delhi.

Fishman, J. A. (1999), Hand-book of Language and Ethnic Identity, New York: OUP.

Kangas, T. S. (1999), Education of Minorities, New York: OUP.

Majumdar, D. N. (1958), Races and Culture in India, Bombay: Asia Publishing House.

National Policy on Education (1986), MHRD, GOI, New Delhi.

National Policy on Education (1968), Ministry of Human Resource Development, Government of India, New Delhi.

Nehru, Jawaharlal (1954), 'Forward' to Elwin, V., Philosophy for Tribal Development, New Delhi.

Patnaik, N. (1982), Tribal Life in Orissa, Souvenir Orissa Sahitya Academy, Bhubaneswar.

Ratnaih (1977), Structural Constraints of Tribal Education, New Delhi: Sterling Publication.

Rout, P. C. (1989), Tribal Education in Orissa, Bhubaneswar: Eastern Graphics.

Sujatha, K. (1994), Educational Development Among Tribes: A Study of Sub-Plan Areas in Andhra Pradesh, New Delhi: South Asian Publishers.

The Indian Child: A Profile, 2002, Department of Women and Child Development, MHRD, New Delhi.

Wetzlaugk, M. S. (1985), Official Discourse, Pedagogic Practice and Tribal Education: A Case Study in Contradiction, *British Journal of Sociology of Education*.

13

Preparing Teachers for Tribal India

1. Dr. Chandolu Sudarsan Raju
2. Pramod Kumar Narikimelli

ABSTRACT

An attempt is made in this paper to highlight the need for preparing teachers to work for Tribal India, as the teachers are the real directors of tribal school. School is one of the most important institutions in any society. It has to play a crucial role in the building up of the society which builds it. The major problem is that Government often recruits teachers from the urban area to teach tribal children. A report says that only 0.56 per cent of teachers are basically from either Anthropology or Sociology discipline. Majority of the teachers are form non-tribal community. Many of them have studied only in English Medium Schools and they even do not know the regional language properly.

1. Guest Faculty, Department of Psychology, Andhra University, Visakhapatnam, 500 003. AP, India.
2. (Ph.D Scholar), Department of Education, Acharya Nagarjuna University, Nagarjunanagar, Guntur District, 522 510. AP, India.

Even though many NGOs are hiring teachers to teach at tribal schools, many of them don't even have any basic degree in education like B.Ed./D.Ed. some of the teachers are sceptical about the performance of the tribal children. The teachers in the Ashram Schools also are not recruited on permanent basis. They are working on contract basis in the schools.

Further, as regards appointment of teachers more and more appointments should be made from among the tribal population so that the teachers become 'accepted' and they deal with the tribal students by using more motivational approach. The existing teachers should be provided with adequate facilities and they should be properly oriented. It should be a must for the teachers to learn the tribal language and there can also be attempts to writing text-books in tribal languages with culture-based curriculum. Fieldwork in a tribal area is to be made mandatory in the training programme so that the teachers concerned can develop appreciation of the cultural ethos of the tribal life and understand the needs of tribal child.

Keywords: Institution, NGO, Sceptical, Fieldwork.

Introduction

Tribals are at the bottom of social and political ladder in India. Development projects have not only bypassed them, but have often harmed them by taking away their resources on which their livelihood was based. Unless the processes which result in their proletararianization are identified and corrective action taken to prevent it, chances are that new programmes will continue to ignore their interests as in the past. Articulation of such processes will not only lead to appropriate solutions but it also helps in sensitizing field officers who in the past often held a negative stereotype about tribals.

Post-independence, the requirements of planned development brought with them the spectre of dams, mines, industries and roads on tribal lands. With these came the concomitant processes of displacement, both literal and metaphorical – as tribal institutions and practices were forced into uneasy existence with or gave way to market or formal state institutions, tribal people found themselves at a profound disadvantage with respect to the influx of better – equipped outsiders into tribal areas. As tribal people in India perilously, sometimes hopelessly, grapple with these tragic consequences, the small clutch of bureaucratic programmes have done little to assist the precipitous pauperization, exploitation and disintegration of tribal communities.

As a result, tribal communities continue to face education and economic deprivation and lack of access to basic services. Due to the absence of rehabilitation following independence, tribals are dispersed across the country, and live on the periphery further away from urbanisation. As industrialization and urbanisation flourish, infrastructure such as roads, water, electricity are not reaching these tribal localities. Reduced accessibility and connection has further deprived tribals from improving their lives. Additionally, adivasis who have accepted 'facelessness' as the only option for survival often migrate to cities as an attempt to stumble on a job within the mainstream. However, they are often unable to find a place in city slums, due to an entrenched caste hierarchy that is difficult to penetrate.

Realising the need to improve the overall status of tribals, their education has emerged at the forefront of recent development efforts. As a basic component of human development, the 83rd Amendment to the constitution has made free elementary education a fundamental right of all the citizens of India. Successive governments have attempted to balance the inequity in the education system, particularly for the marginalized groups. Acknowledging that tribals comprise the most deprived and marginalized groups with respect to education, a host of programmes and measures have been initiated since India's Independence. With education viewed as a crucial input for total development of tribal communities, elementary education has been made a priority area in the tribal sub-plans since the 5th Five-year Plan (1974-79). As of March 2010, there were 20 million ST children out of a total child population of about 193 million in the age group of 6-14 years in the country.

There have been marked improvements in access, and to some extent in quality of primary education in tribal areas. Education has recently witnessed a rapid transformation, particularly in the areas of access, pedagogic reform and community participation in tribal areas. Emphasis has been on improving access to primary education through schemes of Non-Formal Education (NFE), and attempts to improve quality *viz.*, training, using local teachers, adapting curriculum and providing locally relevant teaching-learning materials to tribal students.

Low literacy rates continue to indicate a need for more holistic support, from health to non-tribal attitudes, thus allowing for delivery of high-quality education. Despite the education initiatives, there is disparity among the states in terms of tribal literacy rates ranging from 82 per cent in Mizoram to 17 per cent in Andhra Pradesh. The ST literacy rate continues to be below the national average of 29.6 per cent, with literacy rates among tribal communities (in particular women) tending to be the lowest 2. There exist areas in the tribal-dominated districts across India that remains largely unserved by primary education facilities. Tribal children tend to inhabit forests and hard-to-reach areas where dwellings are spread and access to good quality education is more limited. Low enrolment coupled with soaring drop-out rates in primary schools exacerbates the problem, which has its origin in a gamut of inter-related cultural and socio-economic variables. Adivasis are associated with a certain stigma and behaviour, which can be partially tackled through a change in mindset among non-tribals.

The implement the objective set forth in Article 46 of the Indian Constitution, after independence, the Government has taken number of steps to strengthen the educational base of the persons belong to the SCs and STs. The following programmes and schemes, either fully or partially devoted to benefit the disadvantaged sections of the society in the sphere of literacy.

Educational Development of SCs and STs in India

- Admission/Tuition fees are exempted in KVs up to class XII, for SC/ST students. They are given concession in fees in National Institute of Open Schooling (NIOS).
- The SC/ST students are given concessional fees to the extent of Rs. 450/- for Secondary Courses and Rs. 525/- for Secondary courses.
- Under the Scheme of "Strengthening of Boarding and Hostel facilities for Girls students of secondary and Higher Secondary Schools", 100 per cent financial assistance is given to voluntary organizations to improve enrolment of adolescent girls belonging to weaker sections.
- NCERT operates 'National Talent Search Scheme' - 1000 Scholarships in Science and Social Science up to doctoral level, in medicine and engineering courses up to second degree level are being offered.
- Among 150 and 75 are reserved for SC and ST students respectively.
- Educational development of SCs and STs is major concern of National Institute of Educational Planning and Administration (NIEPA).
- The Scheme of 'Community Polytechnics' (since 1978-79) undertakes rural/community development activities through application of SC and ST.

Constitutional Provisions for Tribals

The Indian Constitution prescribes protection and provisions for the SCs/STs and other backward classes either specially or by way of insisting on their general rights as citizens with the object of promoting their educational and economic interest and of removing the social disabilities. Some of the constitutional provisions are as follow as: The promotion of their educational and economic interests and their protection from social injustice and all forms of exploitation (Article 46).

Article 46 of the Constitution states that, "The State shall promote, with special care, the education and economic interests of the weaker sections of the people, and, in particular of the Scheduled Castes and Scheduled Tribes, and hall protect them from social injustice and all forms of social exploitation".

Commitment in NCMP

The UPA government has set six basic principles for governance. One of them is "to provide for full equality of opportunity, particularly in education and employment for scheduled castes, scheduled tribes, OBCs and religious minorities". Besides, the National Common Minimum Programme (NCMP) of the PA Government contains following provisions aimed at the welfare and empowerment of these communities:

(a) UPA Government will take immediate steps on reverse the trend of communalization of education that had set in the past five years.

(b) Steps will be taken to remove the communalization of the school syllabus hat has taken place in the past five-years. A review committee of experts will be set up for this purpose.

(c) The UPA will ensure that nobody is denied professional education because he or she is poor.

(d) All reservation quotas, including those relating on promotions, will be fulfilled in a time bound manner.

(e) The UPA Government is very sensitive to the issue of affirmative action, including reservations, in the private sector.

Special Provisions

After independence, the Government of India has taken number of steps to strengthen the educational base of the persons belonging to the Scheduled Castes and Scheduled Tribes. Pursuant to the National Policy on Education - 1986 and the Programme of Action (POA) - 1992, the following special provisions for SCs and STs have been incorporated in the existing schemes of the Departments of Elementary Education and Literacy and Secondary and Higher Education:

(a) Relaxed norms for opening of primary/middle schools; a primary school within one km walking distance from habitations of population up to 200 instead of habitations of up to 300 population.

(b) Abolition of tuition fee in all States in Government Schools at least up to the upper primary level. In fact, most of the states have abolished tuition fees for SC/ST students up to the senior secondary level.

(c) Incentives like free textbooks, uniforms, stationery, schools bags, etc., for these students.

(d) The Constitutional (86th Amendment) Bill, notified on 13 December 2002, provides for free and compulsory elementary education as a Fundamental Right, for all children in the age group of 6-14 years.

(e) *Sarva Shiksha Abhiyan (SSA):* SSA is a historic stride towards achieving the long cherished goal of Universalisation of Elementary Education (UEE) through a time bound integrated approach, in partnership with States. SSA, which promises to change the face of elementary education sector of the country, aims to provide useful and quality elementary education to all children in the 6-14 age groups by 2010. The main features of the programme are:

   (i) Focus on girls, especially belonging to SC/ST communities and minority groups.

   (ii) Back to school campus for out of school girls.

   (iii) Free text-books for girls.

   (iv) Special coaching remedial classes for girls and a congenial learning environment.

   (v) Teachers' sensitisation programmes to promote equitable learning opportunities.

(*vi*) Special focus for innovative projects related to girls education.

(*vii*) Recruitment of 50 per cent female teachers.

District Primary Education Programme (DPEP)

The thrust of the scheme is on disadvantaged groups like girls, SCs/STs, working children, urban deprived children, disabled children, etc. There are specific strategies for girls and SCs/STs; however, physical targets are fixed, in an integrated manner including coverage of these groups as well. According to a study by NIEPA, schools in DPEP districts had more than 60 per cent students belonging to SC/ST communities.

Mahila Samakhya (MS)

Mahila Samakya is working with a thrust on SCs and STs. Mahila Samakya addresses traditional gender imbalances in educational access and achievement. This involves enabling women (especially from socially and economically disadvantaged and marginalized groups) to address and deal with problems of isolation and lack of self-confidence, oppressive social customs and struggle for survival, all of which inhibit their empowerment.

National Programme for Education of Girls at Elementary Level (NPEGEL)

The NPEGEL under the existing scheme of Sarva Shiksha Abhiyan (SSA) provides additional components for education of girls under privileged/disadvantaged at the elementary level. The Scheme is being implemented in Educationally Backward Blocks (EBBs) where the level of rural female literacy is less than the national average and the gender gap is above the national average, as well as in blocks of districts that have at least 5 per cent SC/ST population and where SC/ST female literacy is below 10 per cent based on 1991.

Shiksha Karmi Project (SKP)

Shiksha Karmi Project aims at universalisation and qualitative improvement of primary education in remote arid and socio-economically backward villages in Rajasthan with primary attention to girls. It is noteworthy that in Shiksha Karmi Schools, most of the students are from SCs, STs and OBCs.

Kasturba Gandhi Balika Vidyalayas

Under the scheme of Kasturba Gandhi Balika Vidyalaya, 750 residential schools are being set up in difficult areas with boarding facilities at elementary level for girls belonging predominantly to the SC, ST, OBC and minorities. The scheme would be applicable only in those identified Educationally Backward Blocks (EBBs) where, as per census data 2001, the rural female literacy is below the national average and gender gap in literacy is more than the national average. Among these blocks, schools may be set up in areas with concentration of tribal population, with low female literacy and/or a large number of girls out of school.

Jan Shikshan Sansthan (JSS)

The Scheme of JSS or Institute of People's Education is a polyvalent or multifaceted adult education programme aimed at improving the vocational skill and quality of life of the beneficiaries. The objective of the scheme is education, vocational and occupational development of the socio-economically backward and educationally disadvantaged groups of urban/rural population particularly neo-literates, semi-illiterates, SCs, STs, women and girls, slum dwellers, migrant workers, etc. Literacy campaigns have had an enormous impact on other social sectors. The campaigns have served the cause of promoting equity and social justice in society and fostering of a scientific temper and a sense of belonging to India's great composite culture and consciousness of unity in diversity.

Kendriya Vidyalayas (KVs) and Navodaya Vidyalayas (NVs)

Reservation of seats in favour of children belonging to SCs and STs is provided in proportion to their population in the concerned district provided that no such reservation will be less than the national average of 22.5 per cent (15 per cent for SCs and 7.50 per cent for STs seats are reserved for SCs and STs respectively in fresh admissions.) and a maximum of 50 per cent for both the categories (SCs and STs) taken together. These reservations are interchangeable and over and above the students selected under open merit. No tuition fee is charged from scheduled Caste and Scheduled Tribe students up to class XII.

Scholarship Scheme for SC/ST Candidates

Dr. Ambedkar National Scholarship Scheme for meritorious students, is implemented by Dr. Ambedkar Foundation set up under the aegis of the Ministry of Social Justice and Empowerment in 1992 with a view to recognise, promote and assist meritorious students belonging to Scheduled Caste and Scheduled Tribe for enabling them to pursue higher studies. This is one time cash award and will be given to three students scoring highest marks in the regular class X level examination conducted by the Education Board/ Council. This will be separate for SC and ST.

In case none of the first three eligible students are girls, the girl students scoring the highest mark will get a special award. As and when asked by the Ministry of Social Welfare and Justice, NIOS is supposed to send the names of eligible candidates for this scheme. Under the Scheme of strengthening of Boarding and Hostel Facilities for Girl Students of Secondary and Higher Secondary Schools cent per cent financial assistance is given to Voluntary Organizations to improve enrolment of adolescent girls belonging to rural areas and weaker sections.

Preference is given to educationally backward districts particularly those predominately inhabited by SCs/STs and educationally backward minorities. Out of 43,000 scholarships at the secondary stage for talented children from rural areas 13,000 scholarships are awarded to SC/ST students subject to fulfilment of criteria laid down.

Teacher Training and Pedagogy

Teacher absenteeism continues to be a major issue in tribal areas due to long commutes and low motivation levels.

Teacher absenteeism in tribal areas is high as teachers most often live in cities. Children are taught using a city syllabus, which is less applicable to tribal areas, leaving children in a state of confusion. At the same time, teachers, when they are present, are often unclear about the teaching methodology, and do not offer flexibility and freedom to students.

The major problem is that Government often recruits teachers from the urban area to teach tribal children. A report says that only 0.56 per cent of teachers are basically from either Anthropology or Sociology discipline. Majority of the teachers are form non-tribal community. Many of them have studied only in English Medium Schools and they even do not know the regional language properly.

A teacher (whether tribal or not) has to be empowered in both content and methodology. Children are taught by teachers who may or may not be from the tribal community. The presence of tribal teachers, especially from the same community, has shown and improved school participation of tribal children, as these teachers understand and respect the culture with greater sensitivity. Assuming that tribal teachers are a more natural fit, many states have appointed community teachers or para teachers. However, cases have indicated that special training – on both course materials as well as appropriate conduct with tribal students has to be undertaken – even if the teacher has tribal origins.

Why is there a Need for Attitudinal Training of Teachers?

In a discussion of the status of primary education in tribal areas of Orissa, the following reactions from teachers were noted-which are widely applicable across the country (Mishra, 2007). Teachers' behaviour towards tribal children warrants the need for attitudinal training. Tribal children are docile. Non-tribal children are good in Mathematics. Tribal language is not the language of power. Tribal language is not spoken or used by others. Tribal language is parochial and not recognised. Spoken language is limited to the community. There is no grammar in the spoken language. Tribal language is inferior to the regional language. Tribal girls are slow in comprehension compared to boys.

Training and capacity building has to be undertaken on a sustained basis to ensure continued motivation on the part of teachers. Studies suggest that teacher motivation contributes more to the teaching-learning process than teacher competence. There is a need to evolve a sensitive model of tribal education rooted in the psychological strengths of tribal children. For maximum effectiveness, teacher training has to be an ongoing process and not a one-time effort. In addition to training, capacity building of teachers on academic competence and pedagogy is needed.

Elements of Teacher Training and Pedagogy

- *Action:* Training on Material Use: Orientation on local tribal dialects and use of local material for TLM, development of resource training manuals to assist in classroom teaching, tribal primers can be supported by picture dictionary, teacher's hand-book, conversational chart and self-learning materials for teachers and training in the use of interactive, child-centric and gender – sensitive methods of teaching in multi-grade classrooms.
- *Impact:* Increase efficacy of teaching methods and learning.
- *Action:* Changes in Perception of Teachers about Tribal Children: Sensitization to cultural and behavioural strengths of tribal children, emphasis on attitudinal training of teachers and increase motivation levels so teachers can generate interest among tribal children towards education by attempting to link contents of curriculum with existing realities of tribal communities.
- *Impact:* Promote sense of competence, self-efficacy and positive self-image among tribal children changes in perception of teachers about Tribal Children.
- *Action:* Participatory Method of Teaching: Instead of a teachers monologue, encourage students to ask questions, learn through projects/tours, involve students to complete activities prescribed in the syllabus. Follow up

on a student's performance with remedial classes, and adopt a process of continuous evaluation is required. Emphasise holistic education developing social, moral and spiritual values.

- *Impact:* Increase motivation and interest levels of children; enable children to explore creativity and hone managerial/ organizational skills.

Teacher Training Initiatives

Bodh, a Jaipur-based NGO running primary schools for deprived children in rural and urban areas, undertakes capacity building workshops on a monthly basis. Bodh also organizes a 26-day long annual capacity building workshop, where teachers meet to discuss the year's progress, key issues and chart out work plans for the upcoming academic year.

SVYM started the Viveka Teachers Training and Research Centre with the idea of developing model teachers, and creating a research facility to face challenges in the field of education. A semi-residential college offering the Diploma in Education (D.Ed.) course of Government of Karnataka was also started in 2006, catering to 100 students. The course, which is open to students who have passed Class 12 examinations, runs for two years and the first batch, will graduate in October 2008.

RIVER provides hands-on training, on the job support and monitoring, training programmes and materials (teachers manuals, trainers modules, films) etc.

SSA provides central funds for ongoing in-service training of teachers; however there is little information on programme quality and impact of training programmes.

The Education and Technology Services Division implemented a teacher training programme in 454 tribal schools with over 60,000 children in Gujarat. Initiated since 2008, each school requires a minimum of 12 visits per academic session.

Gyan Shala emphasises extensive and concurrent teacher training and support that includes 10-15 day training during bi-annual vacations, monthly one-day refreshers, and weekly demonstration/supervision visits by a senior-teacher/ supervisors.

Research has shown that it is important to train the teachers in the use of dictionaries, flash cards and innovative teacher learning material. Assam was the first State to prepare teacher training modules and separate teaching learning materials for the Bodo tribal language in 1995. Through the DPEP and SSA, Orissa has adopted measures to improve the quality of education in select tribal districts in the state, including developing primers for Classes 1 and 2, following rigorous teacher training programmes. It has trained 350 master trainers on pedagogic issues in the tribal context from selected tribal blocks (Mishra, 2007). On similar lines, Jharkhand undertook a project to ensure that the materials created are utilised effectively.

Creating and Utilising Tribal Material in Jharkhand

"Now that the curriculum is more child-centred, there is a requirement for onsite teacher training, for more support for teachers" SSA Scheme.

There are 29 schedule tribes and 8 primitive tribes in the state of Jharkhand, each tribe boasting their own social customs, language and dialect. In order to bridge the language gap between teachers and students, the project aimed to bring tribal children into the mainstream educational scenario by making them learn the Hindi language as a medium of instruction. Development of appropriate curriculum is a futile exercise in the absence of appropriate training in the use of materials.

1. Preparation of Material

Preparation of reading and writing materials in 4 tribal languages for younger children belonging to different tribal groups, Holding a series of workshops to develop study materials with the final aim of mainstreaming tribal children into the school education system an Using tribal vocabulary and phonetics and linking it with the Devnagri script. (Devnagri script in materials and words taken from the mother tongue)

2. Sensitization of Teacher and Community

Developing training module to sensitize teacher and community towards needs of tribal children and training of resource persons and teachers at the district level.

3. ***Creating Material for Teachers***

Creating materials for teachers outlining the socio-cultural background of tribal people, Material incorporates simple small sentences and words for learning, aimed at teachers unaware of the local language.

4. ***Training on Use of Supplementary Material***

Conducting five-day training on material developed in tribal language for teachers and resource persons, Objective is to develop a proper understanding and imparting knowledge about use of the materials.

Suggestions

This paper suggests that a methodical change is needed in the way teacher perspective, thinking about STs Education and functioning of policy. Foremost provide adequate knowledge in teachers about available schemes for ST children. Their approach must change from simply method of knowledge to practical oriented. The new approaches should help to inculcate the teacher training curriculum and syllabus to promote the awareness of policies and knowledge based advocacy.

Policy-makers, teachers, teacher educators, politicians and educationalists would be taken ST education in all levels seriously. Those who are working in the field of education sector by other ministries only if it does evidence based advocacy by analysing delivery of polices in not up to mark. Government should also set up a group of experts to review the implementation of policies for STs.

Although effective learning for a child rests on the methodology of teaching and the relevance of the content/ curriculum, a teacher is the glue holding these pieces together. A teacher is looked upon as the role model for a child, particularly in the early years, and can often play the part of a surrogate parent. A child's self-image, sense of competence, and self-efficacy can be enhanced – or broken – by a teacher's behaviour in the class environment.

Teachers, both tribal and non-tribal, need to be provided with attitudinal training while dealing with tribal children, as well as guidance on both the use of educational materials and participatory teaching methods. Monetary (higher pay, free transportation etc.) and non-monetary (training, state recognised tribal teaching awards etc.) incentives need to be offered to teachers that are working in tribal areas. Although creating teacher motivation is difficult, high motivation levels are necessary to generate interest among tribal children towards education by attempting to link contents of curriculum with existing realities of tribal communities.

Conclusion

STs in India are marginalized, undernourished and underdeveloped. The basic necessities of a large section of the people belonging to these communities are even remained unfulfilled. When the basic needs are not fulfilled the fulfilment of the needs of the next level of the hierarchy is impossible. Under the condition of extreme poverty and total ignorance, they are found to be exploited by the others. Exploitations of the STs Take many forms and they themselves are not even aware that they are exploited.

Even the Planning Commission does not monitor regularly the impact of existing policies on the ST education and pull up the concerned Ministries. There seems to be an obsession in Government of India with financial budget and not with the impact that policies and programmes have on the marginalized peoples. Policies, programmes and budgetary provisions, despite the rhetoric, have not been integrated so far. Changes in policies and programmes or laws, are not seen as an integral part of the development and planning in India are associated with spending of money. The Planning means expenditure, and this will lead to development is the mindset behind such beliefs. The Indian planner unfortunately has still to understand the difference between planning and budgeting. This is where a systematic change needed in India. In addition to spending budgets, we need to give equal importance to no-monetary issues such as training, state recognised tribal teaching awards etc. The educators, the educational administrators and the people as a whole should support this and devote their time, energy and resource to make this policies and programmes of STs Education as a success. This step of change not only comes from making the policies of Government but also should take care at gross root level proper implementation.

REFERENCES

Dash, A. K. (1989), *Some Leading Issues in Tribal Development,* in M. K. Raha and C. Coomar Tribal India, Gyan Publishing House: New Delhi.

Educational Resource Unit. (2006), *"Inventory of Innovative Practices to Strengthen the Public Education System with Special Attention to Children at Risk."* Commissioned by Department of Elementary Education, MHRD, GOI and International Labour Organization: New Delhi.

Government of India. 2007. Annual Report (2004-05), *Department of School Education and Literacy and Department of Higher Education.* MHRD: New Delhi.

Jharkhand Education Project Council. *"Bridge Material for Tribal Children". Schooling for Special Focus Group.* (http://www.jepc.nic.in/Schooling_of_Special_Focus_Group.html)

Mishra, M. 2007. *"Status of Elementary Education in Tribal Areas of Orissa".* Department of Tribal Education, Orissa.

NCERT. 2007. *Seventh All India School Education Survey - Schooling Facilities in Rural Area.* NCERT: New Delhi.

Nair, P. 2007. *"Whose Public Action? Analysing Inter-Sectoral Collaboration for Service Delivery: Identification of Programmes for Study in India",* International Development Department, Economic and Social Research Council. February.

Sarva Shiksha Abhiyan. 2002. *"Education of Tribal Children in India".* Commissioned by Department of Elementary Education, MHRD: New Delhi.

14

Tribal Education in Iran
Status and Future Perspective

1. Mehdi Mehri Shahabadi
2. Sima Joneydi
3. Dr. Mahsa Moshfegyan

ABSTRACT

Iran is a developing country made up of different tribes, races and cultures. According to the third section of Article III of Iran's constitution, one of the basic functions of the government is to provide public and free education for all students in Iran from different tribal and religious affiliations up to high school level. Iran's educational system has succeeded in eradicating the illiteracy of large number of tribal people. But it was stopped at the initial level of training those people to read and write. Much of these illiteracy fighting efforts were done by the Literacy Movement.

1. Research Scholar, Department of Education and Extension, University of Pune. Email: Mehran_dez_1359@yahoo.com, mehdims@unipune.ac.in
2. Research Scholar, Department of Education and Extension, University of Pune. Email: Sima_joneydi@yahoo.com
3. Email: moshfegyanmahsa@yahoo.com

The literacy Movement Organization (LMO) has been established after the Islamic revolution in Iran in 1980 to contribute to the governmental efforts to eradicate illiteracy. This organization was active in many provinces in Iran. Due to the great role of education in improving the quality of life and qualifying tribal societies for better future, it was necessary for the education system to match its objectives with the societies' needs. The main objective of this research is to study the current status of education in the Iranian tribal areas and to identify the required plans and actions to ameliorate tribal education. This research is meant to highlight the positive aspects of the educational systems applied there and provide suggestions to address their deficiencies. Expanding full-time classes for students and their parents, teaching of ranching, agriculture, general hygiene and medical information, using new technologies – in spite of some current problems and barriers – are some effective approaches in tribal education.

Keywords: tribal, education, perspective, Status, Illiteracy.

Introduction to Iranian Tribal

Like any other community, tribal history is a range of community history. Iran is a country with (an ancient civilization and the people with the wide variety of ethnic and cultural community. Different tribes live in Iran. Great breadth and diversity of climates within the normal time for residents of these areas has created various problems. Each tribe is made up of several smaller tribes. Due to some reasons such as kinship, social and political hardships made by those who are living together in a certain geographical area which is their territory. Different clans in a tribe share the same dialects, customs, traditions and way of life. They form major part of Iran's population of 25 million people who live in rural areas and villages. Farming, rearing and keeping livestock, and producing handicrafts are their main occupations. Since this population is scattered around the country and lives in remote areas and difficult terrain, it makes it really difficult for the government to provide them with services.

Many tribal populations are nomadic, semi-nomadic or sedentarized who are still to be found in Iran, mostly in the southern part of the country where conditions are more like deserts but where the climate is not as harsh as the north. However, the Shahsavan tribe lives in the northwest and the Bodjnurd Kurd, the Sarakhsi and the Sangsari tribes, to mention only the chief ones, in the north-east. Among the many southern tribes, the most important are the Qashgai, Bakhtiari, Lurs, Baluchi and the Kohkilooyeh group. (Varlet and Massoumian, 2011).

The tribal population of Iran is based on general census have been divided to 9 tribes and 547 races. (Iravani, 2011).

History of tribal Education is short along with very Ups and Downs. Rapid changes in the scientific aspects of the previous era's formal education led to the Iranian tribe's education. Widespread illiteracy in the various Iranian tribes forced to offer different policies. Iranian tribes affected by the efforts of an elite education and scientific character. The first school was established in 1951 with the efforts of Mohammad Bahman Beigi who established mobile schools. Mohammad Bahman Beigi set out 78 mobile schools in rural areas. There were classes up to fourth and fifth grade and the ninth grade was mobile as they were boarding. The formal education of tribal law in 1955, created a new chapter in Iranian tribal education. Teacher Training was established nomadically. It was one of the tangible results.

Later an ex-peace corps officer calls the tribal schools, the most exciting successful educational experiment in modern Iranian history. Literacy movement founded after the Islamic Revolution of Iran (1979) has been an attempt to solve the problem of illiteracy in Iranian tribal system.

Tribal and Outlying (Impassable) Schools in Iran

Education in Iran is highly centralized. According to the third section of Article III of Iran's constitution, one of the basic functions of the government is to provide public and free education for all students in Iran from different tribal and religious affiliations up to high school level. Nevertheless, education system has attempted to meet the requirements for basic training which are reading and writing. Providing education for all ethnic groups and tribes living in all regions of Iran is a fundamental task of Iran's government.

Education Literacy refers to people who have the ability to read and write a simple script. They may not have a formal degree. The ultimate goal of eliminating illiteracy from tribal society is the educational system in Iran but apparently it quantitative growth in tribal education more than anything else is of interest to decision makers in the educational system. Available statistics show understanding and importance of literacy among all segments of society.

There are 5934 schools for people living in tribal and impassable areas. 1849 of these schools are temporary tent and Hut schools (Shed) that include 31 per cent of the tribal schools in Iran. These schools are also called white schools. (Vafa, 2009).

Outlying areas have faced the same problems in Iran. Economic and cultural poverty, Low number of students, multiple classes and lack of training facilities and teacher shortage are some of the problems of elementary schools. Installation of container is a way for removing tents from the tribal areas. Tents or container as primary schools are often

the last academic level of student tribes in Iran. Although efforts to promote students' academic conditions are current but still these efforts have failed to overcome this challenge. One of the most important problems in the field of tribal education is high rate of school dropout. Maybe it is hard to accept the fact that more than 58 per cent of students drop out of school. Established management schools outlying is as a step towards increasing the influence rate of Education. There are many outlying areas.

Establishing an independent office of remote regions (outlying) in 2011 and separating it from the nomadic and tribal office have made positive perspective in education of these areas.

A solution is an established boarding school in the tribal areas. These schools are often established in villages. Boarding schools for secondary and high school courses are formed. Boarding schools have been founded at first for youth literacy tribes in Iran. This approach is highly valued, especially in the decades after the revolution. 175 boarding schools in 18 provinces of Iran are active. This figure includes 12 per cent of the high school student population in tribes. These types of schools have access to suitable educational facilities and ICT. Students of these schools mostly have access to teachers, administrative staff and very good service.

Status of Education in Iranian Tribal

Education in Iran is highly centralized and is divided to K-12 education and higher education. K-12 education is supervised by the ministry of education and higher education is under supervision of ministry of science and technology. Primary school (*Dabestan*) starts at the age of 6 and continues for 5 years. Middle school, also known as orientation cycle (*Rahnamayi*), goes from the sixth to the eighth grade. High school (*Dabirestan*), for which the last three years is not mandatory, is divided between theoretical, vocational/technical and manual, each programme with its own specialties.

According to census, 63 per cent of the Iranian tribe's populations are literate. However, the rate of tribal literacy is very low compared with national rate which is 93 per cent. The tribal population of the country based on general census 2008 has shown that more than 56 per cent of the tribal population belongs to the age group of 6-30 years. It shows that tribal population of Iran is very young Iranian. (Iran, 2008).

The age group of 10 to 14 years, with 90 per cent of the highest literacy rates than are other age groups. At present 45 per cent of the population aged 6 to 24 years of Iranian tribes in various academic levels are studying. According to census in 2011, schools faced substantial growth in enrollment of students in the years 2010 and 2011. This amount was equivalent to 50 per cent and it is a major leap in the evolution of tribal education of Iran. Iran's tribal student population in last year was as follower:

Table 14.1: Distribution of the Tribal Students

No.	Academic Level	Population (Thousand)
1.	Elementary schools	125
2.	Middle schools	35
3.	High school and college	12

91 per cent of schools in tribal areas are managed coeducation. 14 thousand teachers are teaching and education faces a shortage of three thousand teachers in the department. Of these, 44 per cent were female and 75 thousand students are included.

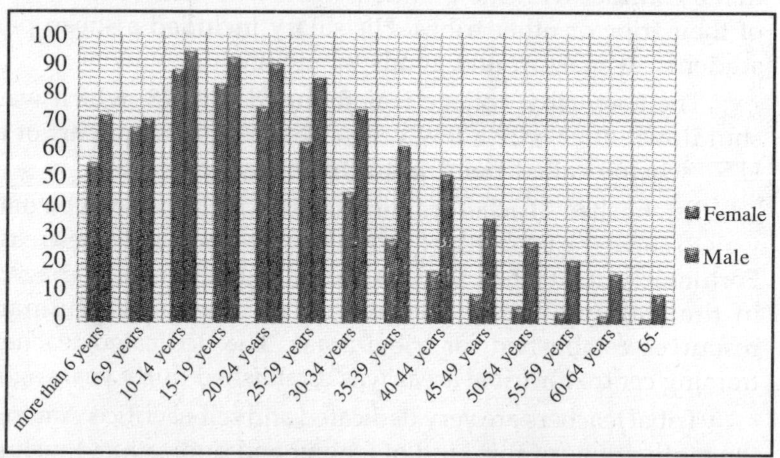

Graph 14.1: Distribution of the Tribal Literacy

The tribal population is very young as shown by the graph and the age pyramid. The literacy rate among the age group 6 to 30 years is high. But the important point is hidden in the definition of literacy.

As stated literacy definition referrers to people who have the ability to read and write a simple script. The primary purpose of Iran educational system is eradicating illiteracy. Thus providing a basic education to all children aged 6 to 14 years is preferred.

The government of Iran has also launched the programme in 2000. This programme has covered uneducated, unskilled adolescents, unemployed educated and women in order to promote their literacy level and life skills. (Zolfaghari, Shatar Sabran, and Zolfaghari, 2009) Significant growth of quality and quantity in rate of tribal education in recent years is clear yet the high rate of dropouts indicates a failure in the main goal. Comparing the rate of literacy among academic levels of tribal students with national rates can find out the short-comings.

Tribal Teachers

Before the start of the new school method, Tribal people made contract with the literate person who calls him 'Molla' of their tribe or other tribes. His salary included a sheep per students, wheat, annual goods or money.

The first tribal college was founded in 1978, which was shut down after only a few years. These centres are part of a U.S., scheme called point four. (Shahshahani, 1995).

Established Teacher training centres for tribes can be one way to solve the problem of shortage of teachers in these areas. Fortunately, in 2009, both boys and girls teacher were triaged in the training centre in order to train required human resources established for tribal areas. The dedicated teacher training centre for tribal areas was established thirty years ago.

Tribal teachers are very dedicated and self-sacrifice. Among the motivations of this kind of feeling and dedication, kinship and tribal and family relationships with the teachers and the students, being relatives and family serving can be mentioned. Tribal teachers love their jobs; it is a religious duty and moral obligation for them as a member of a nation. They count their pupil's fate and students' success as their pride. Teacher tribes are only savior of students from the clutches of ignorance and illiteracy, because student's parents are often illiterate.

Currently 14,593 people are employed as teachers in tribal area. 9801 persons are formal or contract teachers.

Table 14.2: Distribution of the Tribal Teachers

	No. of Teachers	Qualification				Gender	
		Diploma	Associate Degree	Bachelor	Master	Male	Female
Elementary schools	6107						
Junior schools	2420	30.22%	40.6%	28.42%	0.77%	83.54	16.45
High school and college	1274						
Total	14593	4410	5924	4147	112	12192	2401

1. Some of the measures to attract, train and retain human resources in tribal education have done, are as follow:
2. Quota allocated to the tribes and the tribes of the children according to educational level, gender and tribal areas in each province.
3. Two centres dedicated to tribe teachers for male and female.
4. Development of curriculum for teacher training centres, including sociology, nomadic tribes, tribal ecological, approach administration of few basic classes, history and tribal education.
5. Providing, preparing and sending several books and special requirements.
6. Paying one month salary extra to those teachers who have migrated with the tribe.
7. Felicitating those active in the field of science, culture and arts festival and encouraging the individual tribes and inviting other tribes to participate in tours.
8. Universities developing several initiatives in order to promote tribe teachers knowledge (Saydaie, 2003).

Lack of facilities, unpaved roads, and long distances, arduous of the area, lack of encourage and absence of appropriate financial services, missing families, lack of educational materials, teaching aids and facilities, and many other factors are some reasons of teachers being unwilling to teach in these areas and other problems have led to the lack of retention of teachers in these areas. Teachers mostly are soldiers or teachers contract with minimum salaries that have to work in these areas. (Saidaei, 2007).

Educational Programmes and Curriculum

As it was mentioned above, the quality of tribal education has not received any attention from side of the researchers. There has not been no regular evaluation of the quality and impact of tribal and nomadic education for and on the pupils or the local communities. Educational programmes and curricula designed and developed by centres are familiar for most students of the urban areas. Occasionally are not proportional customs and beliefs of the rural and tribal areas indigenous or different. Personal and social experiences of students in rural and tribal areas are different and it makes their learning process difficult.

For example, the language used at schools and homes in the community with dialog language is different. Reasons unrelated to the subject of life in the villages and tribes, the urbanisation trend have been intensified.

Common Problems of Iranian Tribal Education

Issues of tribal education can be divided into two categories:

(i) ***Problems of Tribes Living Conditions***

1. Distribution and low population tribes accommodation.
2. Role in the production of children as human resources: By 2007, Iran had a student to workforce population ratio of 10.2 per cent, standing among the countries with highest ratio in the world.
3. Financial problems of tribal people.
4. Away from urban centres and industrial and lack of transportation.
5. Lack of awareness and lack of access to information and communication technology (ICT).

6. Problems related to bilingual and local tribal dialects.
7. Resistance to the changes.
8. Traditionalism and patriarchy.
9. Parental illiteracy and lack of need for literacy.
10. Sudden vamoose.

(ii) Problems Associated with the Education System

1. The lack of School and junior high school at the tribal settlement centres is one of the dissatisfactions of the tribal population.. (Saidaei, 2007).
2. Mismatch between the course content and books with tribes living conditions.
3. Lack of necessary and appropriate educational environment.
4. Shortage of teachers in tribal area (Abasi, 2007).
5. Multiple base classes.
6. More attention to the quantitative issues in education.
7. Co-education.
8. Mobile tent schools and Sheds.
9. The lack of research in the field of tribal education.
10. Lack of infrastructure technology such as light, phones, computers...

(Journal of Johad: The basic problems of the tribal: Take cultural and social issues of education).

Conclusion

Shortage of teachers in tribal area is one of the challenges of educational system. Undoubtedly courage, financial charge and providing welfare facilities of tribal teachers in order to full attending and living in tribal areas will solve some problems. Establishing vocational institutes related to the Ranching and Agriculture as most profession of tribal people can be a factor of students dropout rate. The literacy Movement Organization (LMO) contributes to the state efforts to eradicate the illiteracy but this organization could not repeat its success in part of tribal education. As mentioned earlier, tribal schools require classroom-based instruction requiring substantial investment in facilities such as buildings, furniture, teachers, teaching aids, and facilities. Expanding full-time classes for students and their parents, teaching of ranching, agriculture, general hygiene and medical information, using new technologies secondary schools; eradicating gender and regional inequalities in education; meeting the changing learning needs of tribal children, youths and adults adequately, also providing functional vocational education including income generating skills that can engender self-employment and thereby raise their incomes and standards of living. (Danaher, Kenny, and Leder, 2009).

In the absence of a trend of urbanisation in Iran's tribal life, it is quite tangible and the number of Iranian tribe students greatly reduced in school classroom and leads to increases of the cost of education in this section so The emphasis on the use and Developing Information and Communication Technology (ICT) Can be the key to solving many problems in this section.

REFERENCES

Abasi, L. (2007), Study of The Yield of the Desired Status and Learning in Rural and Tribal Education. Tehran: Iranian Students' News Agency - ISNA.

Danaher, A. P., Kenny, M., and Leder, J. R. (2009), Traveller, Nomadic and Migrant Education. New York, NY 10016: Routledge.

Iran, S. C. O. (2008), Economic and Social Survey of Migratory Tribal 2008 (No. 1), Tehran: Department of Planning and Strategic Supervision.

Iravani, M. (2011), The Method of Increment and Improvement of Tribes' Education (Quantity and Quality) (Case Study on Arab Tribes in Jarghooyeh). *International Journal of Applied Science and Technology*, Vol. 1 (No. 5), 83-87.

Saidaei, E. (2007), Study the Main Issues of Nomads Centres and Provide Scientific Solutions Applicable. *Journal of Geographical Research*, 97, 139-166.

Saydaie, S. E. (2003), Sustainable Development among the Bakhtiari Tribe, Nomadic Peoples. Issue, 7(2), p. 70-78.

Shahshahani, S. (1995), Tribal Schools of Iian: Sedentarization through Education. *Jorunal of Nomadic People*, 36(37), 145-156.

Vafa, J. (2009), Qualitative and Quantitative Problems of Education in the 21st century. Afarinesh. Retrieved from F:\Tribal Education\detail.asp.htm

Varlet, H., and Massoumian, J. (2011), Education for Tribal Populations in Iran. 2012, from http://www.greenstone.org.

Zolfaghari, A., Shatar Sabran, M., and Zolfaghari, A. (2009), Community Learning Centres Programme as an Educational Tool for Community Literacy Development in the Islamic Republic of Iran: Community of Golshan as a Case Study. *Asian Social Science* (CCSE), Vol. 5 (No. 8), 60-66.

15

Socio-Economic Status of Katkari Community in Thane District
An Overview

1. Grishma Manikrao Khobragade

Introduction

The post – independence period in India, Indian Government planned and formulated the policy of rural development. The word rural development suggests overall development of rural areas to improve the quality of life of rural people. In this context, it is a broad and multi-dimensional perception, and includes the development of agriculture and related activities, village and cottage industries and socio-economic infrastructure, and connected activates and facilities and above all, human resources in rural areas.

Village India is not seen as united and harmonious but divided by caste and class conflict and the force of change being brought about in society were the result of a change in relations and modes of production. Tribals in India were never a problem for themselves or others prior to the colonial-

1. Assistant Professor, Department of English, Birla College, Kalyan, (Affiliated to University of Mumbai) (M. S.) E-mail: khobragade.grishma@yahoo.com. Mobile: 9869530720.

modern attack. India is known for its village and rural areas. Small and marginal farmers, landless labours, fisher folk etc., constitute the poor in rural areas. Many of them belong to socially deprived castes and tribes such as Katkari, schedule tribe. The dominant castes, landlords, rich peasants, money lenders, merchants (sawakar) etc., exploit and subjugate them. The present study grasps the features of Katkari community in Thane District. The study deals with socio-economic problems of Katkari community and the social, cultural factors which Katkari community suffers from. The major objectives of the study are as under:

Objectives of the Study

1. To understand the status of Katkari community in Thane District in order to know the basic needs of life required for their socio-economic development.
2. To describe the importance of their socio-economic problems.
3. To study the their skills and life style.

Methodology

The present study is carried out with the support of primary and secondary sources of data .The secondary sources are related websites, Books and Records.

Discussion

Katkari is the ancient Tribe in Thane District in Maharashtra along with Madhia Gond and Kolam. Katkaris are socially and economically backward in the process of development. A number of tribal communities such as Thakur, Mahadev Koli, Katkari, Warli, Kokna, etc., live in Thane District. Most tribal groups are socio-economically marginalized. Their livelihoods are totally dependent on agriculture and forests. Most of them are small and marginal farmers or landless labourers. Men-women and children work as bonded labour on brick kilns in far away places. Lack of food security, malnutrition, starvation deaths, land alienation, low land holdings, unemployment, depleting natural resources, drinking water contamination and shortages, lack of to proper health care facilities, socio-political marginalization, etc., are some of the major issues in the tribal context in Thane Districts of Maharashtra.

The name Katkari is derived from their profession of making 'Kath' or catechu from the Khair tree (Acacia catechu). Katkaris are known for their physical strength, endurance and hunting-gathering skills. The entire Katkari tribe has been experts in specific professions. For instance, the occupation of making Kath was a specialty of Katkaris. The number of Katkaris practicing this trade gradually declined as the population of Khair trees went down and a ban was imposed on the cutting the tree (around 1968). The Katkaris then collectively became expert charcoal makers until the Government of Maharashtra banned the making of charcoal from wood (around 1985). It was at this point of time that the Katkaris turned towards brick making. Today the Katkaris are considered expert brick makers and the entire group is engaged in this profession. They continue to work as bonded labour for their savkar (owner or landlord). Their exploitation by non-tribal is total and absolute. The police department harasses and treats them like a *'criminal tribe'*. Katkaris are the modern slaves in 21 century. All schemes for development, programmes, Government or Non-Government, bypass the Katkaris. Nobody seems to be bothered about the unique and different Katkaris. The land on which a village is located is called Gaothan. It is legal ownership of the village land or Gaothan. But it is found that many villages, the ownership of Gaothan is either with the Forest Department, or moneylenders. Hence Katkari families living in such villages always live under the burden of the landowner. They can neither build better houses nor avail of any Government programmes for basic amenities like drinking water, etc., in villages. The landowner does not permit them to do anything on the land, and on the contrary, forces Katkari families to move by harassing them. Katkaris are cheated, exploited and made to work under sub-human conditions on the brick kilns (furnace). Over 90 per cent of the Katkari families are landless and are totally dependent on wage labour for their livelihood. The exploitation by brick contractors, harassment by police administration and absolute neglect by government have left hardly any space or scope for the Katkaris to survive in present world. The community lives in miserable poverty and despair.

Their source of revenue is totally on agriculture and forests. Most of them are small and minor farmers or landless labourers. Forests provide an uncultivated food (vegetables, fish, and birds) for use as well as gum, mahua flowers, tendu patta, honey, wild fruits, etc. The availability of forest produce has declined considerably due to deforestation. This has an adverse effect on the food security and livelihood of tribals. There is no employment opportunity in the region apart from cutting trees for forest contractors or working as labourers in fields or on government jobs.

Income source is limited to maintain their status. Money is a limited product and quite often tribal do not have sufficient money other things like marriages, building house, illness etc., are even more difficult to deal with the common matters.. They have to take money from moneylenders at very high interest rates. Tribals often find it difficult to repay the moneylender's loan.

Katkari's one family makes about 1,500 bricks per day. The Katkaris work for 6 days in a week, cases, even holiday is not allowed. In a month, the Katkaris produce about 36,000 bricks. It can be said that a family makes about 30,000 bricks in a month. At Rs. 160 for thousand bricks, each family should earn up to Rs. 4,800 per month. Katkaris work for 6 to 7 months on brick kilns. So in a year, each family should earn something like Rs. 29,000 to 33,600 working on brick kilns. In fact, the Katkari family gets Uchal (advance) of Rs. 2,000 to 3,000 once in a year and Kharchi (wages) of Rs. 250 to 300 per week. That is, Rs. 1,000 to Rs. 1,200 per month or Rs. 6,000 to Rs. 7,200 in wages over a period of 6-7 months. The advance and the interest are constantly deducted from wages. Considering an advance of Rs. 3,000 and wages of Rs. 7,200; a Katkari family gets poorly paid by anywhere between 19,000 to 23,400 in a year. The Katkaris have contributed, literally brick by brick, to build and rebuild major urban centres like Mumbai, Pune, Panvel, New Mumbai, Thane, Kalyan, etc. However, the brick project has not given them anything in return, apart from exploitation and bondage.

Most of the Katkari families are poor and landless. There are a few families who have own land but do not have any paddy fields. In fact, Katkaris have not paid attention towards farming and cultivating. A few of them have been cultivating crops on forest land. Tribals are the original residents of this land, but today they are landless and staying on land owned by someone else. They have wonderful knowledge about uncultivated foods like fish, crabs, animals, birds, wild vegetables, fruits, nuts, etc. It is really wonderful to see Katkari women drawing out crabs from their holes during summer months by rubbing two stones to imitate the sound of cloudbursts. It is a great skill to understand the hunting-gathering skills of Katkaris and the results provide a remarkable insight into the originality and knowledge of Katkaris for survival. Katkaris continue to be hunter-gatherers when they are not working as bonded labour on brick kilns. Katkaris are expert fishermen, swimmers, divers, archers. They are famous for their strength, stamina and hunting-gathering skills. Katkaris are experts in stone crushing, tree cutting. Some of the families are engaged in these trades for employment (and survival). However, in all these vocations, Katkaris are not paid proper wages and treated as bonded labour. The Katkaris are labourers and firewood sellers. Their women are hard workers and help them by hawking head loads of firewood. Physical appearance of Katkaris is much darker and slimmer than the other forest tribes. Katkari women are tall and slim, unclean and uncombed, and the children can always be known by their thin and stressed look. They have no peculiar language and show no signs of ever having had one.

Katkari are depending on other community. The most of the Katkari villages are situated close to non-tribal villages since these provide some wage opportunities. Katkari houses are a low roof thatched with grass. The houses are very small. Their huts are of mud with a peaked roof thatched with palm leaves. There is generally a separate cook-room. The only equipment is a few earthen pots and pans, several hens and dogs, a few fishing traps, perhaps a bow and arrows, and a couple of stones for crushing kusai seed. They eat every sort of flesh, except the cow and the brown faced monkey. Houses and surroundings are dirty and unclean. The men wear a blanket, and some tattered cloth round their heads. They are very poor, being much given to drinking, and passing days together without food.

There is no unity in society. Katkaris is unorganized hence they can easily exploit by the other forces. State government does not attention to their problems because they do not have a political will to help the community since Katkaris do not form a major vote bank. There are many other factors contribute to the lifelong poverty and marginalization of Katkaris. Katkaris are cheated, exploited and made to work under sub-human conditions on the brick kilns. Sexual exploitation of Katkari women is common while men are often beaten up, and even killed. Whenever Katkaris try to protest against the exploitation, brick kiln owners file cases of robbery and theft against the Katkari families in the police station. Katkari families always remain under the control of the land owner or the forest department. The owner does not allow them to build better houses or to develop a drinking water source by digging a well. In some Katkari villages there are instances of the land owner harassing Katkari families who were provided improved houses by the Government (under the Indira Awas Yojana).

The Katkari families took away the roofing tiles from their houses and migrated to another village. In another place, a non-tribal person from the neighboring village claimed that the village land belonged to him as soon as a tar road was built up to the Katkari village. Katkaris hence always live under fear and terror. The problem of land ownership in tribal settlements needs to be resolved on a priority basis.

Government programmes for the upliftment of tribal communities (mainly the Integrated Tribal Development Programme - ITDP) bypass the Katkaris. Interestingly, a large number of Katkari villages are not eligible for support under ITDP since they are located outside the Tribal Sub Plan (TSP). Katkaris are forced to stay outside the TSP for reasons of employment from non-tribal villages.

Conclusion

There is an urgent need to initiate comprehensive development work for the Katkari community. While efforts are needed at several fronts, a proper survey of all Katkari families and hamlets is a priority. It also needs to be understood that any development work with the Katkari community would be a fairly long term affair, given their socio-economic status and level of marginalization. Development interventions for Katkari would have to consider the following:

- Ownership of land on which their village is located (Gaothan).
- Ownership of agricultural land to landless Katkari families (forest encroachments, ceiling lands, encroachments by outsiders on ceiling lands).
- Help to take up agriculture and land-based livelihoods (land improvement, tree planting, etc.,).
- Better houses.
- Livelihood skills.
- Useful employment.
- Drinking water sources near villages.
- Better and meaningful education for children.
- Improved access to health care.
- A legal study of the historical aspects pertaining to the identification of Katkaris as a 'criminal tribe'; the present-day consequences; reasons for harassment of Katkaris by the Police; and necessary corrections in the judicial and police systems to prevent atrocities and harassment of Katkaris.

- Treatment of Katkaris on par with other citizens of the country; with assured human and other rights.

There are many other related issues that need to be addressed. As an organization working with tribal communities in Raigad and Thane Districts, There are a few NGO like ADS is deeply concerned about the plight of the Katkaris. Academy of Development Science (ADS) is NGO involved in work with Katkaris in Raigad and Thane District. It is unfortunate that the Government seems to be least bothered about the plight of the Katkari community. The lack of information about development status, socio-economic indicators, health and nutrition status, etc., amongst individual tribal groups is a serious lacuna in Government policy. The economic situation of tribals may not be as important in the integration and mainstreaming efforts.

REFERENCES

"Gazetteer of the Bombay Presidency, 1883".

www.ashanet.org/projects/project-view.php?p=325

www.rainforestinfo.org.au/katkari/index.html

16

Higher Education to Empower Tribal

1. Dr. Sunita G. Hiremath

ABSTRACT

The importance of education has been stated by 'India Vision 2020' stating that education is important for the growth of the society as well as for the individuals. Properly planned education input can contribute to increase in the gross national products. Cultural richness build positive attitude towards technology and increase efficiency and effectiveness of governance. Education opens new horizons for an individual, provides new aspirations and develops new values. It strengths competencies and develop commitment. India is democratic country. For the very success of democracy it is of prime importance that the people are educated and aware of their duties as well as rights. India is a country of middle class where all cannot send their wards to universities and colleges due to their low income.

1. Associate. Professor, Maeer's Mitscoe, M.Ed. Sec. Kothrud, Pune. E-mail: sunitamalkothe@gmail.com

So every possible effort should be there to make education within the reach of common man. Thus, higher education should not be for rich and creamy class but for all. Articles 330, 332, 335, 338 to 342 and the entire Fifth and Sixth Schedules of the Constitution deal with special provisions for implementation of the objectives set forth in Article 46. These provisions need to be fully utilised for the benefit of these weaker sections in our society.

The paper attempts to know and understand the challenges in tribe's education. The main aim of this paper is to study the initiatives taken by UGC for reform in higher education of tribes. The present paper also put insight on assessment of the efficacy of the programmes and policies meant for education of tribes.

Keywords: Higher education, Schedule tribes, Policies.

Introduction

India is democratic country. For the very success of democracy it is of prime importance that the people are educated and aware of their duties as well as rights. They must be trained to avoid violence and handle the situation in an amicable way for the welfare of entire society. India is a country of middle class where all cannot send their wards to universities and colleges due to their low income. So every possible effort should be there to make education within the reach of common man. Thus, higher education should not be for rich and creamy class but for all. Article 46 of the Constitution states that, "The State shall promote, with special care, the education and economic interests of the weaker sections of the people, and, in particular of the Scheduled Castes and Scheduled Tribes, and shall protect them from social injustice and all forms of social exploitation". Articles 330, 332, 335, 338 to 342 and the entire Fifth and Sixth Schedules of the Constitution deal with special provisions for implementation of the objectives set forth in Article 46. These provisions need to be fully utilised for the benefit of these weaker sections in our society. The Government has special concern and commitment for the well-being of the Scheduled Tribes who suffer as a Group due to their social and economic backwardness and relative isolation.

The total number of tribal communities recognised by the government as Scheduled Tribes is 572 in number. Scheduled Tribes are those tribal communities who have been listed so by the President of India in keeping with Articles 341 and 342 of the Constitution. These tribal communities mainly live in Scheduled Areas, or those outlying areas, which during the British times did not come under the direct purview of civil, criminal and revenue administration. The tribes are scattered in all States and Union Territories in India except for the states of Haryana, Punjab, Delhi, and Chandigarh. The tribes are heavily concentrated in the northeastern states of Arunachal Pradesh, Meghalaya, Mizoram, and Nagaland although they constitute a small percentage of the total tribal population in India.

The Distribution of Tribal Communities in India

- *North-Eastern Region:* In the mountain valleys and other areas of north-eastern India, covering the States and Union Territories like Arunachal Pradesh, Assam, Manipur, Meghalaya, Mizoram, Nagaland and Tripura live tribes like the Abor, Garo, Khasi, Kuki, Mismi, Naga, etc., who mostly belong to Mongolian race and speak languages belonging to the Tibeto-Chinese family.
- *Himalayan Region:* In the sub-Himalayan regions covering parts of North-Bengal, Uttar Pradesh and Himachal Pradesh live tribes like Lepcha, Rabha, etc., mostly belonging to Mongolian racial group.
- *Central India Region:* In the older hills and Chotanagpur Plateau, along the dividing lines between peninsular India and the Indo-Gangetic basin, live many tribal communities like the Bhumij, Gond, Ho, Oraon, Munda, Santal, etc., covering the States of Bihar, Orissa, Madhya Pradesh and West Bengal and mostly belonging to Proto-Australoid group.

- *Western India Region:* Covering the States like Rajasthan, Maharashtra, Gujarat, Goa, Dadra and Nagar Haveli live a number of tribal communities the most important of them being the Bhil racially belonging to the Proto-Australoid group.
- *Southern India Region:* This region falls south of the river Krishna. Covering the States of Karnataka, Andhra Pradesh, Tamil Nadu and Kerala, in the Nilgiri Hills and converging lines of the Ghats live the Chenchu, Irula, Kadar, Kota, Kurumba, Badga, Toda, Malayam, etc., having Negrito, Caucasoid, Proto-Australoid or mixed physical features.
- *Island Region:* Covering Andaman, Nicobar and Lakshadweep Islands live a number of small tribes like the Andamanese, Onge, Sentinelese, etc.

Objectives

1. To know problems of tribe's education.
2. To describe the schemes and policies for educational advancement of the scheduled tribes.
3. To assess the efficacy of the schemes and policies meant for education of tribes.
4. To study the initiatives taken by UGC for reforms in higher education of tribes.

Limitations

- It is only limited to documentary sources and does not throw any light on people's perceptions of these schemes and policies.
- Lack of availability of material with the Government offices corporations and departments on the subject is another serious limitation.

Delimitation

The study was limited to content analysis of objectives taken for the study.

Methodology

Documentary analysis method was employed. The present study is exploratory in nature, with the purpose of describing the various schemes and policies for educational advancement of the scheduled tribes.

Data Collection

Books on higher education in India, Education of tribes were collected for the present study. The present study is based on only documentary sources, since it does not cover the people's perceptions regarding these schemes and policies. The published material, available in the form of books, journals, seminar papers, plan documents, annual departmental reports, etc., have been used as documentary source. However discussion has been held with the officials and subordinate personnel involved in the implementation of these schemes and programmes.

Tools of the Study

Various reports and documents were surveyed for getting adequate information on the subject. In order to present these schemes and policies in chronological order, departmental progress reports have also been surveyed. Discussions with knowledgeable persons have also been held in order to get needed clarifications in various published and unpublished documents related with the subject.

Data Processing

The collected material has been edited and classified as need.

Analysis and Interpretation

The edited and classified material has further been analysed and interpreted logically, keeping in view the objectives of the present study.

Conclusion Related to First Objective

To Know and Understand Problems of Tribe's Education

There are many problems in the education of scheduled tribes which are listed bellow:

(a) Late start of formal education.

(b) To send grown up boys and girls is an economic problem to a tribal family as it entails dislocation in the traditional pattern of division of labour.

(c) The schools are at some considerable distance from home.

(d) Inadequate number of educational institute and inadequate hostel facility.

(e) Language is major barrier in the initial schooling stage of tribal children.

(f) Unsuitable curricula and text-book for lower classes.

(g) Teacher in the tribal areas come mostly from non-tribal areas. In many cases they lack necessary understanding of the people and their culture. As such they do not devote themselves to their work with the required enthusiasm.

(h) Extreme poverty, illiteracy, ignorance and exploitation of tribes are other causes for educational backwardness of scheduled tribes.

Conclusion Related to Second Objective

To Know Schemes and Policies Regarding Tribe's Education

Following three types of schemes have been organized by the government for the scheduled castes and tribal people.

1. The work directly done by the central government.
2. The work done under the supervision of the central government.
3. The work done by the various states in the country.

Major schemes and policies are as bellow:

(a) **Post Matric Scholarship (PMS) for Scheduled Tribes Students**

The Scheme has been in operation since 1944-45.

Objective

The objective of the scheme is to provide financial assistance to students belonging to Scheduled Tribes pursuing Post-Matriculation recognised courses in recognised institutions. The scheme covers professional, technical as well as non-professional and non-technical courses at various levels and the scheme also includes correspondence courses including distance and continuing education. The scheme is implemented by the State Government and UT Administrations, which receive 100 per cent Central Assistance over and above the committed liability which is required to be borne by them from their own budgetary provisions. The committed liability is equal to the expenditure reached in the last year of the Plan period.

Salient Features

(i) The students are provided different rates of scholarships depending on the course. The courses have been divided into four categories and the rates vary from Rs. 140/- per month to Rs. 740/- per month. Besides, the compulsory fees are also being reimbursed.

(ii) There is provision for readers' allowance for visually handicapped students and escort and transport allowance for physically handicapped students, study tour charges, thesis typing/printing charges, book allowance to students pursuing correspondence course and compulsory non-refundable fees charges by the educational institutions.

(iii) The scholarship covers the whole duration of the course and is paid on an annual basis and is subject to the satisfactory performance of the student and good conduct.

***(b)* Book Bank**

Objective

Many ST students, selected in professional courses find it difficult to continue their education for want of books on their subjects, as these are often expensive. In order to reduce the dropout rate of ST students from professional institutes/ universities, funds are provided for purchase of books under this scheme.

Salient Features

The scheme is open to all ST students pursuing medical (including Indian Systems of Medicine and Homeopathy) engineering, agriculture, veterinary, polytechnic, law, chartered accountancy, business management, bio-science subjects, who are receiving Post-Matric Scholarships.

(i) The books, for the purposes of the Book Banks scheme are restricted to prescribed text-books.

(ii) One set of books is purchased for two students of all professional courses except in respect of post-graduate courses and chartered accountancy where one set is purchased for each student.

(iii) The books making one set in each course is decided by an Expert Committee constituted by the State Government for each course.

(iv) The life period of each set of books is fixed at 3 years.

(v) The central assistance to States/UT Administrations for setting up Book Banks is limited to the following ceiling or actual cost of the set, whichever is less.

(c) **Up-gradation of Merit of ST Students**

It has since been functioning only as a sub-scheme of the PMS. The Scheme was revised with effect from the financial year 2008-09.

Objective

The objective of the scheme is to upgrade the merit of ST students by providing them remedial and special coaching in classes IX to XII. While remedial coaching aims at removing deficiencies in various subjects, special coaching is provided with a view to prepare the students for competitive examinations for seeking entry into professional courses like Engineering and Medical disciplines. The scheme provides for 100 per cent central assistance to the States/UT's. A package grant of Rs. 15,000/- per student per year is provided and the State/UTs are not required to bear any financial burden. Besides the amount of scholarship, students with disabilities are also eligible for the following assistance:

(a) Reader Allowance of Rs. 100 per month for blind students in classes IX to XII.

(b) Transport allowance of Rs. 50 per month for the disabled student if such a student does not reside in the hostel, which is within the premises of educational institution. The disability as per the said Act is defined as blindness,

low-vision, leprosy-cured, hearing impairment, locomotors disability, mental retardation and mental illness.

(c) Special pay of Rs. 100 per month is admissible to any employee of the hostel willing to extend help to a severely orthopedically handicapped student residing in a hostel managed by the educational or by the State Government/ Union Territory Administrative who may need the assistance of a helper.

(d) Escort allowance of Rs. 50 per month for severely handicapped day scholar students with lower extremity disability.

(e) Allowance of Rs. 100 per month towards extra coaching to mentally retarded and mentally ill students in classes IX to XII.

The provisions proposed in *(a)* to *(e)* above, also apply to leprosy cured students.

Salient Features

(i) The State Government/UT Administration select certain schools in different Districts/towns with hostel facilities which show excellence in performance of students from class IX to XII. The Ministry fixes the total number of awards for each State annually.

(ii) Coaching starts from class IX in the identified schools and continues till the awardees complete class XII.

(iii) Coaching is provided in languages, science, mathematics as well as special coaching for admission to professional courses like engineering and medicine.

(iv) While selecting the ST students the aim is to include at least 30 per cent girl students and 3 per cent disabled students.

(v) A revised package grant of Rs. 19,500/- per student per year is provided from 2008-09 which includes the honorarium to be paid to the Principal or Experts imparting coaching and also to meet incidental charges.

(vi) Students with disabilities are provided additional grants.

(vii) 100 per cent financial assistance is provided to the States and UTs for implementation of the scheme.

(d) Centrally Sponsored Scheme of Girl's and Boy's Hostels for Scheduled Tribes

The scheme for Construction of ST Girls' Hostels was started during the Third Plan period. A separate scheme for Construction of Hostels for Scheduled Tribe Boys was launched in 1989-90. Both schemes were merged into one scheme during the 10th Five-year Plan. The Scheme was revised with effect from the financial year 2008-09 (w.e.f. 01-04-2008).

Objective

The objective of the scheme is to promote literacy among tribal students by providing hostel accommodation to such ST students who would otherwise have been unable to continue their education because of their poor economic condition, and the remote location of their villages.

Salient Features

(i) The scheme provides for the construction of new hostels and extension of existing hostel buildings for the middle, secondary, college and university levels of education.

(ii) The State Government/UT provides the land for the building, free of cost.

(iii) The scheme does not provide recurring expenditure for the running of the hostels.

(iv) The maintenance of the hostels and the regulation of their use is done by the State Government/implementing agencies.

(e) Rajiv Gandhi National Fellowship Scheme (RGNF)

This Scheme was introduced in the year 2005-06. Every year 667 fellowships are to be provided to ST students. The maximum duration of a fellowship is 5 years. The scheme is being implemented by University Grant Commission (UGC) on behalf of the Ministry of Tribal Affairs. Any ST student who has passed post-graduation from a UGC recognised University can apply under the scheme.

Objective

The objective of the scheme is to provide fellowships in the form of financial assistance to students belonging to the

Scheduled Tribes to pursue higher studies such as M.Phil. and Ph.D.

Amount of Scholarship Per Student

Sl. No.	Item	Amount
1.	Fellowship	@ Rs. 8000/- p.m. for initial two years (JRF) @ Rs. 9000/- p.m. for remaining tenure (SRF)
2.	Contingency for Humanities and Social Sciences	@ Rs. 10000/- p.a. for initial two years @ Rs. 20500/- p.a. for remaining tenure
3.	Contingency for Sciences	@ Rs. 12000/- p.a. for initial two years @ Rs. 25000/- p.a. for remaining tenure
4.	Departmental assistance	@ Rs. 3000/- p.a. per student to the host institution for providing infrastructure.
5.	Escorts/Reader Assistance	@ Rs. 1000/- p.a. in case of physically and visually handicapped candidates
6.	House Rent Allowance	As per the UGC pattern

Salient Features

(i) Under the Scheme 667 fellowships will be provided to the ST students each year.

(ii) The maximum duration of the fellowships is 5 years.

(iii) Fellowships are provided to ST students to enable them to pursue higher studies such as M.Phil. and Ph. D.

(iv) Implementation shall be by UGC on behalf of the Ministry of Tribal Affairs.

(v) There will be no restrictions as regard to the minimum marks in the Post Graduation Examination or prior clearance of NET examination.

(f) Establishment of Ashram School in Tribal Sub-Plan area

The scheme is operational in tribal sub plan States and UT Administration since 1990-91. The Scheme has been revised with effect from the financial year 2008-09 (w.e.f. 01-04-2008).

Objective

The objective of the scheme is to promote and extend educational facilities to Scheduled Tribe students including PTGs. Ashram Schools provide education with residential facilities in an environment conducive to learning.

Salient Features

(*i*) The scheme provides funds for the construction of school buildings from the primary to the senior secondary stage and also provides for the up-gradation of the existing Ashram Schools for Scheduled Tribes Boys and Girls including PTGs.

(*ii*) Under the scheme, besides school buildings, the construction of students' hostels and staff quarters are also undertaken. The State Government/UT provides the land for the Ashram Schools, free of cost.

(*iii*) Financial assistance on 50:50 basis is also provided for other non-recurring items of expenditure like the purchase of furniture, equipment, sets of books for the school library, etc.

(*iv*) Only the capital cost is provided under the scheme. The recurring expenses are to be met by the State Governments.

(*v*) The location of new schools and admission policy should be decided by State/UT.

(*vi*) The Ashram Schools shall be completed within a period of 2 years from the date of release of the central assistance. However for the extension of existing Ashram Schools period of construction is 12 months.

(*g*) **Vocational Training in Tribal Areas**

This scheme was introduced in 1992-93; revised with effect from 1.4.2009 and is being implemented through the State Governments/UT Administrations, Institutions or Organizations set up by Government as autonomous bodies, educational and other institutions like local bodies and cooperative societies and Non-Governmental Organizations etc. The capacity of each vocational training centre is 100 with hostel facility for 50. Each centre may cater to five vocational courses in traditional or other skills depending upon the employment potential of the area. Each tribal boy/girl is trained in two trades of his/her choice, the course in each trade being for duration of three months. Each trainee is attached at the end of six months to a Master Craftsman in a semi-urban area for a period of six months to learn his skill by practical experience, the practical experience in each trade being of three months duration. There is provision for monthly stipend and for raw material for the trainees.

Objectives

The main aim of this scheme is to develop the skill of the tribal youth in order to enable them to gain employment/self-employment opportunities.

Salient Features

(i) The scheme will be implemented for the benefit of the Scheduled Tribes as well as PTGs and can be taken up anywhere in the country but priority will be given to remote tribal areas, areas inhabited by particularly vulnerable tribes and areas affected by extremist activities.

(ii) Under the scheme, the training for trades including modern trades having employment potential in the region should be provided.

(iii) This scheme is exclusively for the benefit of scheduled tribes as well as PTGs. The organization running VTC will admit the ST youth irrespective of the region/State to which they belong.

(iv) As far as possible, minimum 33 per cent seats will be reserved for tribal girl candidates.

(*h*) Scheme of Coaching for Scheduled Tribes

The scheduled tribe candidates coming from deprived families and disadvantaged environment find it difficult to compete with those coming from a socially and economically advantageous background. To promote a more level playing field, and give ST candidates a better chance to succeed in competitive examinations, the Ministry of Tribal Affairs supports a scheme for coaching for disadvantaged ST candidates in quality coaching institutions to enable them to successfully compete in examinations for jobs/admission to professional courses.

The scheme supports free coaching to scheduled tribe students for various competitive examinations *viz.*, Civil

Services/State Civil Services/Other Exams conducted by UPSE like CDS, NDA, etc./professional courses like Medical, Engg., Business Administration/Banking/Staff selection Commission/ Railway Recruitment Boards/insurance companies, etc. The financial norms of the scheme have been revised during 2007-08. The scheme covers coaching fees, monthly stipend @ Rs. 1000/- per ST student per month and boarding/lodging charges for outstation students @ Rs. 2000/- per ST student per month for the period of coaching.

(i) Scheme of Top Class Education for ST Students

Ministry of Tribal Affairs introduced a new scholarship scheme of Top Class Education for ST students from the year 2007-08.

Objective

The objective of the scheme is to encourage meritorious ST students for pursuing Studies at degree and post degree level in any of the selected list of institutes, in which the scholarship scheme would be operative.

Salient Features

- *(i)* The family income of the ST students from all the sources shall not exceed Rs. 2.00 lakh per annum.
- *(ii)* The ST students will be awarded scholarship covering full tuition fee and other non-refundable dues in respect of Government/Government-funded institutions. However, there will be a ceiling of Rs. 2.00 lakh per annum per student for private sector institutions and Rs. 3.72 lakh per annum per student for the private sector flying clubs for Commercial Pilot Training.
- *(iii)* The scholarship also provides for *(a)* living expenses @ Rs. 2200/- per month per student subject to actual, *(b)* books and stationery @ Rs. 3000/- per annum per student and *(c)* cost of a latest computer system along with its accessories limited to Rs. 45000/- as one time assistance during the course.
- *(iv)* The scheme will be funded by the Ministry of Tribal Affairs on 100 per cent basis and the funds shall be released directly to the institution concerned.

(j) National Overseas Scholarship Scheme for Higher Studies Abroad (NOS)

The scheme has been in operation since 1954-55. This was a Non-Plan Scheme, which became a Plan scheme from 2007-08.

Objective

The objective of the scheme is to provide financial assistance to selected ST students pursuing higher studies (Masters, Doctoral and Post-Doctoral level) in certain specified fields of Engineering, Technology and Science only.

Salient Features

(i) The scholarship is awarded to ST candidates (one member from each family) below 35 years of age on the date of advertisement, provided the total income of the candidate or his/her parents/guardians does not exceed Rs. 25,000/- per month.

(ii) For a Post Graduate course the candidate shall possess 1st Class with 60 per cent marks or equivalent grade in the relevant Bachelor's degree with at least 2 years' work experience being desirable; for M.Phil./Ph.D. course he/she shall have a 1st Class with 60 per cent marks or equivalent grade in the relevant Master's degree with 2 years' research/teaching/work experience being desirable. For Post-Doctoral studies a candidate shall have 1st Class with 60 per cent marks or equivalent grade in the relevant Master's degree and Ph.D. 5 years' teaching/research/professional experience in a relevant field is desirable.

(iii) The candidates are required to arrange admission to a university/institute abroad on their own within 3 years from the date of communication of selection.

(iv) The awardees are provided a maintenance allowance of US$ 14,000 or £9000 per annum, which they may supplement up to US$ 2400 or £1560 per annum, by undertaking research/ teaching assistantship. In the event of earnings beyond this limit, the Indian Mission may reduce the maintenance allowance granted under the scheme correspondingly.

(*v*) The awardees on return to India have to remain in India for at least 5 years.

(*k*) Strengthening Education among Scheduled Tribe Girls in Low Literacy District

It is a gender scheme of the Ministry. The scheme aims to bridge the gap in literacy levels between the general female population and tribal women, through facilitating 100 per cent enrolment of tribal girls in the identified Districts or Blocks, more particularly in naxal affected areas and in areas inhabited by Primitive Tribal Groups (PTGs), and reducing drop-outs at the elementary level by creating the required ambience for education. The scheme recognises the fact that improvement of the literacy rate of tribal girls is essential to enable them to participate effectively in and benefit from, socio-economic development.

The scheme covers 54 identified districts in 12 States and 1 Union Territory where the ST population is 25 per cent or more, and ST female literacy rate is below 35 per cent or its fractions, as per 2001 census. In addition, any other tribal block in a district, other than aforesaid 54 identified districts, which has scheduled tribal populations 25 per cent or above, and tribal female literacy rate below 35 per cent or its fractions, as per 2001 census, are also covered. The scheme also covers PTG areas and gives priority to areas affected by naxalism. The scheme is implemented by non-governmental organizations (NGOs) and autonomous societies of the State Governments/ Union Territory.

The scheme primarily envisages the running and maintenance of hostels linked with schools running under Sarva Shiksha Abhiyan or other schemes of Education Department. Where such schooling facilities are not available, the scheme has provision for establishing a complete educational complex with residential and schooling facility. The scheme has provision for tuitions, incentives and periodical awards to encourage the ST girls.

Conclusion Related to Third Objective

To Assess the Efficacy of the Schemes and Policies Meant for Education of Tribes

The success of any policy is contingent upon its effective implementation. The review of the implementation of the schemes and policies would be undertaken by the Ministry of Tribal Affairs, once a year, within 3 months from the close of the previous fiscal year and the findings of the review would be taken into account for effective implementation of the policy.

Some important landmark achievements in education of Tribes are as below:

- 100 Residential Schools proposed to be set up during the 9th Plan period by utilising part of the allocation for grant-in-aid under art. 275(1) of the Constitution, to improve the quality of education being imparted to tribal students. 75 Residential Schools have already been sanctioned, out of which 12 schools are already under operation.
- Funds provided to State Governments/UTs for construction/improvement of about 1400 km of roads in tribal areas, 250 staff quarters for schools, 200 school and hostel buildings 1600 class rooms, 50 community centres, and also for drinking water facility, rural electrification, culverts/cause-ways and rural irrigation projects.
- Post-Matric Scholarship for pursuing post-matriculation courses, including professional, technical and non-professional/non-technical courses extended to Rs. 3.66 lakh ST students during 2000-01.
- During Tenth Five-year Plan, total 29113 ST youths were provided vocational training through State Government and NGO run institutions (21583 youths trained through States and 7530 through NGOs) with a financial support of Rs. 30.63 Corer (Rs. 24.35 Corer to States and Rs. 6.28 Corer to NGOs).
- During Tenth Five-year Plan, 84 educational complexes for Scheduled Tribe (ST) girls were supported in identified low literacy districts through NGOs and autonomous

societies of the State Governments, with an amount of Rs. 33.34 crore which benefited 9646 ST girls.

Conclusion Related to Fourth Objective

To Study the Initiatives taken by UGC for Reforms in Higher Education of Tribes

The following guidelines were given by UGC to introduce a number of positive schemes for better facilities for SC/ST in universities and colleges.

(i) Reservation of admission quota for various courses both at undergraduate and post graduate levels and follow up measures for its implementation in universities and colleges. The reservation for SC/ST students to various courses in colleges and universities have been revised since August 1982. This reservation stands at 15 per cent for SC and 7.51 per cent for ST. This percentage corresponds to the percentage of the SC/ST population in the total Indian population.

(ii) Remedial courses provision of additional guidance/ coaching classes in particular subject.

(iii) Establishment of book banks.

(iv) Preparation of teaching materials.

(v) Assistance to colleges catering to the needs of SC/ST students.

(vi) *Remedial Coaching at UG and PG Level*: UGC in 1994 introduced this scheme. The main objective of the scheme are:

(a) To improve academic skills and linguistic proficiency of the students in various subjects.

(b) To raise the level of comprehension of basic subjects to provide a stronger foundation for further academic work.

(c) To strengthen their knowledge, skills and attitudes in such subjects, where qualitative techniques and laboratory work are involved so that necessary guidance and training provided under the

programme may enable the students to come up to the level necessary for pursuing higher studies efficiently.

(d) To improve overall performance of these students in the examinations.

The tenure of assistance to implement the scheme in universities and colleges is five years but initially assistance is provided for three years, called first phase. The period of assistance is linked with the help of standing committee on SC/ST and if found satisfactory, further extension of two years would be granted to College/University.

(vii) *Scheme of Coaching Classes for Preparation for National Eligibility Test (NET)*: The main objective of the scheme is to prepare SC/ST candidate for appearing in the NET so that sufficient number of candidates become available for selection of lecturer in the University system.

(viii) *Coaching Classes for Entry in Services*: The scheme has been introduced by UGC during 2004-05. The caching scheme is operates at two levels, (1) Coaching for group B and C level posts and (2) All India Services, State/Provincial services.

(ix) *Teacher Fellowship for SC/ST Candidates*: The UGC had a scheme for 'direct Award of Teacher Fellowship' for SC/ST college teachers to do research work leading to the award of M.Phil./Ph.D. degree.

(x) The UGC initiated the scheme of post-doctoral fellowship for SC/ST candidates who have obtained a doctorate degree and have published research work to their credit.

(xi) Post-Graduate Scholarships for SC/ST Students in Professional Courses.

(xii) UGC introduced the scheme of establishment of Special Cells in Universities in the year 1983 for the purpose of co-ordination and implementation of SC/ST schemes.

Functions of the Special Cells

1. To circulate Government of India and Commission's decisions and to collect regularly, on an annual basis,

information regarding course-wise admissions to candidates belonging to the Scheduled Castes and Scheduled Tribes in the Universities and Colleges for different courses, in forms prescribed, by a stipulated date, and to take follow up action, where required.

2. To circulate Government of India orders and Commission's decisions and to collect information in respect of appointment, training of these communities in teaching and non-teaching posts in the Universities and Colleges, in suitable forms by a stipulated date and take follow up action where required.
3. To collect reports and information regarding the Government of India orders on the various aspects of education, training and employment of Scheduled Castes and Scheduled Tribes candidates, for evolving new policies or modifying existing policy by the Commission.
4. To analyse the information collected above and prepare reports and digests for onward transmission to the Ministry of Human Resource Development/University Grants Commission and such other authorities as may be required.
5. To deal with representations received from Scheduled Castes and Scheduled Tribes candidates regarding their admission, recruitment, promotion and other similar matters in Universities/Colleges.
6. To monitor the working of the remedial coaching scheme, if approved in the affiliated colleges and university.
7. To function as a Grievances Redressal Cell for the Grievances of SC/ST students and employees of the university and render them necessary help in solving their academic as well as administrative problems.
8. To maintain a register for employment of SCs/STs in the University and Colleges for the candidates belonging to SC/ST communities for various posts in the university/ colleges.

9. Any other work assigned from time to time to promote higher education among these two communities suffering economic, social and education deprivations.
10. The SC/ST Cell exclusively looks after the work related to SC/STs matters and no other work is assigned to the Cell.
11. If the required data is not submitted by the given date, UGC reserves the right to withhold either plan or non-plan grant until the required information/data is received. Hence, the universities/colleges are advised to supply the necessary information as required.

REFERENCES

http://tribal.nic.in

Kale, R. K. (2005), "Special Schemes of UGC for Empowerment of SC/ST," University News, Vol. 43, No. 47, November 21-27.

Pal, Ompraksh (2011), "Sociological Foundation of Education", APH Publishing Corporation, New Delhi.

Ramaiah, P. (1998), "Issues in Tribal Development", Chugh Publications, Allahabad.

Sharma N. and Thakur A. K. (2010), "Indian Higher Education and Tribals", Deep and Deep Publications, New Delhi.

Verma M. M. (1996), "Tribal Development in India", Mittal Publications New Delhi.

17

Strategies for Promotion of Education among the Scheduled Tribes

1. Dr. K. Devan

Introduction

The spread of education among the weaker sections of our society is vital as education is a prime requisite for socio-economic development. The policy to promote educational interests of the weaker sections of the people, especially the Scheduled Castes and Scheduled Tribes, has been enshrined in our Constitution as a Directive Principle of State Policy. In the days of yore tribal people had a well-organized system of education. The child learnt at home and at 'dormitories' and this training related to various activities of tribal life. But with the advent of Christian missionaries modern schools came up in tribal areas.

Homogeneity is the main characteristic of a tribe; but this characteristic has been dealt a death blow due to the impact of modernity. An implicit stratification system is emerging

1. Associate Professor, Centre for Adult and Continuing Education, Pondicherry University, Puducherry - 605 014.

within the tribal society on the basis of education, income, status and power. On the one hand a few privileged people are reaping all the benefits and on the other the vast bulk of tribals is wallowing in poverty and deprivation. Moreover these educated elites, instead of trying to improve the lot of the underprivileged brethren, are ruthlessly exploiting them. This has led to a situation where the majority of the tribals look upon these educated 'babus' with distaste and distrust and thus it has evoked a negative attitude towards education. With modern education have come modern values which have clashed with the age-old traditional values of tribal society; this has also led to the tribals being antagonistic to modern education.

Thus the teacher feels isolated and unhappy and a disgruntled teacher is, certainly, not the best communicator of modern ideas and messages to tribal children. So even though the government has come up in recent times with various plans and programmes to improve the educational lot of the tribals, there is not much result to show as there is lack of sincerity on the part of the officials charged with the implementation of these programmes. In fact a credibility gap has emerged between such officials and the tribal people. If all these problems are to be tackled successfully, the government has to bring about a change in the basic orientation in tribal education.

The government in its zeal to provide facilities to the tribals has constructed hostels for the tribal students, supplied text-books, provided different types of scholarship, etc. But instead of bridging the gap it has widened the rift. The tribal students staying in separate hostels, availing themselves of separate scholarships, feel naturally ostracised. This should change and instead there might be some percentage reservation of seats for tribals in a general hostel and tribal students should be encouraged to take an active part in various college as well as hostel activities. Only then they could be brought into the mainstream.

It has also been proved that when a tribal child begins his education he starts with no linguistic information and conceptualization whereas a non-tribal child starts with a few familiar concepts and linguistic associations. So preschool training programme for the tribal child is a prime requirement and the government should undertake such programmes if it means to put the tribal students on an equal footing with the non-tribal. As regards appointment of teachers, more and more appointments should be made from among the tribal population so that the teachers become 'accepted' and they deal with the tribal students by using a more permissive and motivational approach. The existing teachers should be provided with adequate facilities and they should be properly oriented. It should be a must for the teachers to learn the tribal language and there can also be attempts at writing textbooks in tribal languages.

The Constitution

The Constitution of India does not define Scheduled Tribes as such. Article 366(25) refers to scheduled tribes as those communities who are scheduled in accordance with Article 342 of the Constitution. According to Article 342 of the Constitution, the Scheduled Tribes are the tribes or tribal communities or part of or groups within these tribes and tribal communities which have been declared as such by the President through a public notification. As per the 1991 Census, the Scheduled Tribes account for 67.76 million representing 8.08 per cent of the country's population. Scheduled Tribes are spread across the country mainly in forest and hilly regions.

The essential characteristics of these communities are:

- Primitive Traits.
- Geographical isolation.
- Distinct culture.
- Shy of contact with community at large.
- Economically backward.

The 1991 Census figures reveal that 42.02 per cent of the Scheduled Tribes populations were main workers of whom 54.50 per cent were cultivators and 32.69 per cent agricultural labourers. Thus, about 87 per cent of the main workers from these communities were engaged in primary sector activities. The literacy rate of Scheduled Tribes is around 29.60 per cent, as against the national average of 52 per cent. More than three-quarters of Scheduled Tribes women are illiterate. These disparities are compounded by higher dropout rates in formal education resulting in disproportionately low representation in higher education. Not surprisingly, the cumulative effect has been that the proportion of Scheduled Tribes below the poverty line is substantially higher than the national average. The estimate of poverty made by Planning Commission for the year 1993-94 shows that 51.92 per cent rural and 41.4 per cent urban Scheduled Tribes were still living below the poverty line.

The Constitution of India incorporates several special provisions for the promotion of educational and economic interest of Scheduled Tribes and their protection from social injustice and all forms of exploitation. These objectives are sought to be achieved through a strategy known as the Tribal Sub-Plan strategy, which was adopted at the beginning of the Fifth Five-year Plan. The strategy seeks to ensure adequate flow of funds for tribal development form the State Plan allocations, schemes/programmes of Central Ministries/ Departments, financial and Developmental Institutions. The cornerstone of this strategy has been to ensure earmarking of funds for TSP by States/UTs in proportion to the ST population in those State/Uts. Besides the efforts of the States/ UTs and the Central Ministries/Departments to formulate and implement Tribal Sub-Plan for achieving socio-economic development of STs, the Ministry of Tribal Affairs is implementing several schemes and programmes for the benefits of STs.

The progress over the years on the literacy front:

	1961	1971	1981	1991	2001
Total literate population	24 %	29.4 %	36.2 %	52.2 %	64.84%
Scheduled Tribes (STs) population	8.5 %	11.3 %	16.3 %	29.6 %	47.10%
Total female population	12.9 %	18.6 %	29.8 %	39.3 %	53.67%
Total Scheduled Tribes (STs) female population	3.2 %	4.8 %	8.0 %	18.2 %	34.76%

There are now 194 Integrated Tribal Development Projects (ITDPs) in the country, where the ST population is more than 50 per cent of the total population of the blocks or groups of block. During the Sixth Plan, pockets outside ITDP areas, having a total population of 10,000 with at least 5,000 scheduled tribes were covered under the Tribal Sub-Plan under Modified Area Development Approach (MADA). So far 252 MADA pockets have been identified in the country. In addition, 79 clusters with a total population of 5,000 of which 50 per cent are schedule tribes have been identified. In order to give more focused attention to the development of Scheduled Tribes, a separate Ministry, known as the Ministry of Tribal Affairs was constituted in October 1999. The new Ministry carved out of the Ministry of Social Justice and Empowerment, is the nodal Ministry for overall policy, planning and co-ordination of programmes and schemes for the development of Scheduled Tribes. The mandate of the Ministry includes social security and social insurance with respect to the Scheduled Tribes, tribal welfare planning, project formulation research and training, promotion and development of voluntary efforts on tribal welfare and certain matters relating to administration of the Scheduled Areas. In regard to sectoral programmes and development of these communities, the policy, planning, monitoring, evaluation as also their co-ordination is the responsibility of the concerned central Ministries/Departments, State Governments and UT Administrations. Each Central Ministry/Department will be the nodal Ministry of Department concerning its sector. Ministry of Tribal Affairs supports and supplements the efforts of State Governments/U.T. Administrations and the various Central Ministries/Departments for the holistic development of these communities.

Strategies

The following strategies are suggested for the development:

- Strengthening Self-Help Groups (SHGs) and other Community-Based Organizations (CBOs) and increasing their capacities and skills in Sustainable Livelihood Management (SLM).
- Providing training programmes to the Non-Government Organizations (NGOs), leaders of the Self-Help Groups (SHGs) on organizational development process (ODP) which is increasing their capacities and skills in addressing development issues and strategies.
- Promoting environment awareness and protecting bio-diversity of the country in association with local self-government/panchayat raj institutions (PRIs).
- Conducting applied action research (AAR), documentation of reports and communication through dissemination.
- Creating a common platform for all the rural and *adivasi* communities to share experiences and exchange best practices in the empowerment fields.
- Working with panchayats, students, farmers, government officers, NGOs for the development of the rural and hill areas through collective action.
- Awareness raising on the importance of the environment, forest resources, medical plants conservation and promotion of best conservation practices.
- Community-based protection of all common property resources for the sustainable development of present and future generations.
- Reducing illiteracy and ignorance and promotion of opportunities with changing learning systems for a changing world with rights based education for all the marginalized.

- Empowering local communities on economic self-reliance with agricultural and allied activates through the promotion of alternatives and innovation livelihoods activities.
- Empowering indigenous communities of India through co-operative action with dignity and identify towards self-reliance and self-determination and self-rule.
- Studies and research activities on development schemes, plans, policies and laws.
- Child rights protection and campaign on school enrolment among the rural and adivasi areas through networking with NGOs, and State Departments.
- Facilitating planning, monitoring, evaluation and learning process with cost-benefit analysis for the NGOs, SHGs, private and public organizations.
- Documentation and publication for the replication of best models towards sustainable development.

Issues that are to be Addressed

- Extreme poverty, hunger and unemployment.
- Displacement, migration and lack of livelihoods.
- Discrimination, exploitation, atrocities and violence.
- Illiteracy, ignorance and lack of educational opportunity.
- Poor health condition, malnutrition and lack of access to health care.
- Gender in-equality and lack of opportunity to women's rights.
- Lack of identity and acceptance to indigenous best knowledge and skills.
- Lack of availability of civil rights and basic needs in all the villages.
- Lack of opportunity in the political sectors and caste/ class discrimination.
- Poor management of natural resources and over exploitation of natural resources.
- Lack of support and co-operation for the agricultural activities.

- Lack of people's participation in the development programmes and plans.

Rights that are to be Focused

- Education and Literacy Rights.
- Economic and Livelihood Rights.
- Health and Housing Rights.
- Environment and Water Rights.
- Gender Equality and Women's Rights.
- Equality and Dignity Rights.
- Political Participation Rights.
- Social justice and Human Rights.
- Culture and Identity Rights.

Areas of Intervention

- Poverty Reduction and Economic Empowerment.
- Gender Equity and Women's Empowerment.
- Civil Rights and Social awareness with Literacy activities.
- Educational Development and Child Rights Activities.
- Environmental Preservation and Conservation Activities.
- Political Participation and Promoting Panchayat Raj Institutions.
- Prevention of Violence Against Women campaign.

Conclusion

Moreover the education of children has little functional importance to them. Even after secondary education there can be no gainful employment. Thus there is no incentive for education. So the existing curricula should be related to socio-economic and cultural life of the tribals. Emphasis must be on imparting skills and modern information on agriculture, poultry, forestry and carpentry, etc. Only by providing better communication facilities, sanitary programmes, teaching materials and methods the government can hope to bring about an attitudinal change in the tribal population towards education. Otherwise with the present state of affairs the dream of our Constitution makers about tribal education would always remain a dream.

Index

Q

R